BANTAM BOOKS

TORONTO • NEW YORK • LONDON • SYDNEY • AUCKLAND

RANGERS

by
James R. Arnold

TEAMWORK:

A ranger sergeant from the 75th Infantry, Airborne Rangers, sprints to a new position while the rest of his men provide covering fire during an exercise designed to test their reactions under simulated enemy fire. Ranger School's tough, vigorous training attracted a special kind of soldier.

PAINT JOB:
A bulky ranger of Company L, (Rangers) 75th Infantry, clasps a tiny vanity mirror in one hand as he starts to apply camouflage before setting out on a night mission during Operation Bushmaster. In the jungle, the art of camouflage was taken seriously.

BACKMARKER:
Looking down the sights of a captured enemy AK-47 assault rifle, a rear scout keeps watch over a trail. Being the backmarker was often the loneliest job on a long-range reconnaissance patrol (LRRP). With his back to the rest of the patrol, a rear scout could quickly become isolated when the action began.

JUNGLE PATROL:
Eyes down and scanning the ground
for the slightest clue of the enemy,
men of Company H, 75th Rangers,
make their way through the jungle.
To a ranger, constant vigilance was
as vital as the M-16 rifle he carried.

THE ARVN:

Men of the 4th ARVN Rangers use all their strength to push a jeep into the cargo hold of a US CH-47 helicopter. While US rangers operated in small, tightly knit teams of five or six men, the South Vietnamese rangers operated in company-sized units.

EDITOR IN CHIEF: Ian Ballantine. SERIES EDITORS: Richard Grant, Richard
Ballantine. BOOK EDITOR: John Forbes. PHOTO RESEARCH: John Moore.
DRAWINGS: John Batchelor. MAPS: Peter Williams. PRODUCTION: Owen Watson.
STUDIO: Kim Williams.
PRODUCED BY: The Up & Coming Publishing Company, Bearsville, New York.

RANGERS
THE ILLUSTRATED HISTORY OF THE VIETNAM WAR
A Bantam Book/ March 1988

ACKNOWLEDGEMENTS

*The author wishes to thank veterans Woody Arnold, Steve Campbell, Tom
Cueto, and Nguyen An Long for the time they so generously gave, the staffs
of the US Army Center for Military History and the US Army Military
History Institute for their help with research, and Nancy Olds for
photographic assistance.*
*Photographs for this book were selected from the private collections of
Woody Arnold and Steve Campbell and the archives of the US Army Center
of Military History and DAVA.*

LIBRARY OF CONGRESS
Library of Congress Cataloging-in-Publication Data
Arnold, James R.
  Rangers / by James R. Arnold.
    p.   cm.—(The Illustrated history of the Vietnam War)
  ISBN 0-553-34509-5 (pbk.)
  1. Vietnamese Conflict, 1961–1975—Commando operations.
I. Title. II. Series.
DS558.92.A76 1988
959.704'342—dc 19

Published simultaneously in the United States and Canada

PRINTED IN THE UNITED STATES OF AMERICA

CW 0 9 8 7 6 5 4 3 2 1

Contents

Team Opel   17

Learning to survive   29

The buildup   45

Nam's Angels   61

Tracker Force!   83

Hell breaks loose   93

Lessons learned   99

From LRRP to ranger   113

The cowboys   123

Going home   153

Glossary   156

Team Opel

Ranger operations are overt operations by highly trained units into enemy-held areas for the purpose of reconnaissance, raids, and general disruption of enemy operations ... The Ranger Imprint is: Pride, confidence, self-determination, and the ability to lead, endure, and succeed regardless of the odds or obstacles of the enemy, weather, and terrain.

—from the Department of the
Army Field Manual

THE MISSION WAS to enter the mountainous jungle, observe enemy movement, and snatch some prisoners if possible. Previous missions into this area had led to contact with the North Vietnamese. The nine Americans in the team anticipated this mission would be equally eventful. As one ranger said: "After a few missions you get a feeling; you just know they are there."

As the helicopter carries the rangers toward the insertion point on 12 January 1970, the men are unusually nervous. Combat veterans all, they do not startle easily. Previous long-range reconnaissance patrols had given them a life-preserving sixth sense. Now their sixth sense tingles.

While the nine Americans give up trying to shout over the constant noise of the helicopter's rotors, a tenth team member silently waits. Regardless of the noise, he would have had trouble talking to the team. Not only is Vo Can Sau the oldest team member at 33 years of age—most of the others are around 20 years old—but he doesn't speak English. Since none of the Americans speak Vietnamese they are left to guess at Sau's thoughts. A North Vietnamese Army (NVA) veteran for the past 17 years,

Team Opel

MOMENT OF DECISION:
With the safety switches flicked off, a ranger patiently holds the firing handle of a claymore mine as he listens for enemy movement on a nearby trail. One squeeze of the handle and the claymore will erupt with a red-orange flash, emitting a fan-shaped blast capable of killing anything over a 50-meter range. But claymores were not always a reliable line of defense, as the men of Team Opel discovered. Approaching within 15 meters, the NVA discovered and disarmed the team's claymores.

Sau had "rallied" to the Allied cause and is now a Kit Carson Scout. His role is to use his special knowledge of the North Vietnamese to help the rangers perform their mission. As the helicopter flies on, several rangers observe that the normally animated scout is very quiet. This fact, combined with yesterday's combat that had seen two of their ranger comrades killed, makes everyone more nervous than usual.

At 1600 hours they reach the insertion point and

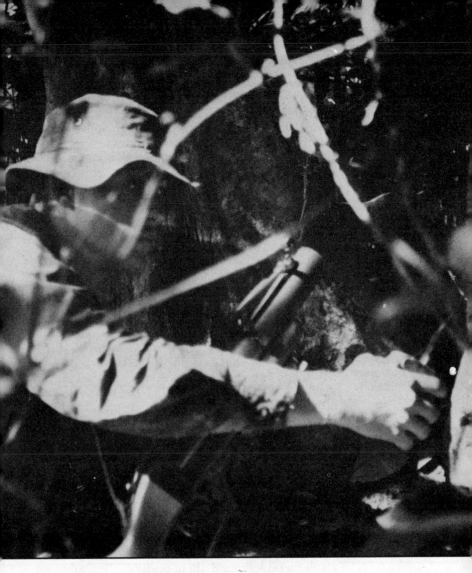

land. The rangers tumble from the helicopter into man-high elephant grass. They quickly set out for their night position, knowing that darkness comes quickly in the jungle. They don't move too quickly though. Vo Can Sau regulates the march, stopping frequently to look and listen. The rangers know that he only displays such caution if he feels the NVA are nearby. Accordingly, the rangers too move cautiously. Advancing up a slope several of them note that if they have to retreat hastily, here are

Last word —A ranger lieutenant gives his squad a final briefing, while one of his men grabs a quick smoke, before moving out on a mission.

several places the NVA could rig an ambush. They remember and move on.

Arriving at their night positions they rig eight claymore mines around their tiny perimeter. The mines serve as their first line of defense. The 10-man team forms a small circle with only some 2 feet between each soldier. Those who have an appetite eat. Jittery stomachs keep most from the food. The unflappable scout starts to smoke a cigarette. Suddenly he puts it out and grabs his rifle. Sau's behavior further alerts the team. The team communicates with him in a mixture of hand signs, facial expressions, pictures, and a few words of Pidgin English.

"Beaucoup NVA?" asks Team Leader Sergeant James Bates.

Nodding affirmatively the scout replies: "Beaucoup NVA."

With this warning the scout has done his job. If he does nothing else on this operation he will have earned his pay, as far as the rest of the patrol are concerned. They have not seen the enemy, but the scout has and that is enough for them. There is nothing to do but wait. Two men are assigned to stay awake. The others sleep fitfully. The whirling buzz of teeming insects and the eerie cry of ninge lizards—whose loud exhale seems to say "fuck you, fuck you"—serenade them.

At 2045 hours they begin to see signs of enemy movement. Voices drift through the jungle, then flickering flashlights appear through the underbrush. The North Vietnamese are on the move. Team Opel tries to radio to base to arrange artillery support. Although they are not supposed to get into heavy combat, advance planning has made sure that if they do have to fight the artillery can put a solid steel curtain around their position. But advance planning has not accounted for a faulty radio. Repeated attempts to link up with the artillery fail. The radio won't work. The 10-man team is on its own.

Down in the valley the sound of an electric generator starting up startles the rangers. Apparently Team Opel has stumbled on an NVA base camp. Periodically the engine cuts off and all the lights wink off. Whenever this happens, a few moments later the sound of aircraft passing

overhead reaches the rangers. When the aircraft departs the engine comes back on and the flashlights reappear. Detection from the air has to be avoided at all costs. If it is not, the North Vietnamese know full well the price they will pay in the form of US air strikes on their position. The rangers eye the planes as a potentially life-saving link with the outside world. But there is no way to communicate with them. Oblivious to the drama on the ground, the pilots speed onward.

As time passes, it seems that flashlights blink all around the rangers' position. Team Opel is surrounded. The sounds of something passing through the jungle draw closer. When the noise approaches within 20 meters the entire team tenses. It is unmistakably the enemy. An NVA soldier appears silhouetted against the horizon. Built almost like an American, he is much larger than the normal Vietnamese. Watching him approach, several rangers begin to pray, silently pleading not to be discovered.

The large enemy soldier comes within 15 meters, then 10. The nearest ranger grips his knife. Another silently aims his rifle at the figure. On he comes. Suddenly a thin beam of light illuminates the terrain. He has turned on a flashlight! With the beam pointing directly at a hidden ranger, the enemy soldier approaches to within five feet. Then he

DISARMED:
A former VC sapper shows concentration as he uses bolt cutters to disarm a claymore mine lashed to a perimeter post. Capable of creating a fan-shaped kill zone with a radius of 50 meters, the wire-operated claymore was widely used as an antipersonnel mine.

freezes. He stands still for a terribly long time. Finally he looks directly at the nearest American, smiles, turns his back, and leaves. If the rangers shoot him the noise will reveal their position. Instead they let him go.

The booming of artillery echoes off nearby hills. It seems to cause the NVA to stir from their valley base camp. In large numbers they begin to move toward Team Opel, apparently forced in this direction by the artillery fire. The entire team expects

Team Opel

VITAL LINK:
A ranger from the 75th Infantry reports contact with enemy forces during a patrol near Uan Loc along the Dong Nai River in 1970. The radio was the rangers' only form of contact during the long days away from base. Without it, as Team Opel discovered, there was no way to summon help or fire support.

an assault at any moment. For two hours it doesn't come.

Instead the acrid smell of marijuana drifts over them. Several rangers think "they're trying to get up enough nerve before they attack." Enemy soldiers come ever closer. The rangers smell their unwashed bodies. The body odor is so intense that, as one ranger swears, he can almost taste it.

Midnight comes and passes and still no attack. The exhaustion brought on by tension and fear causes

Survival weapon —The commando combat knife was a standard. Worn in a sheath holstered over the right shoulder blade for fast access, it served as a useful tool in the jungle as well as being used as a weapon for silent killing.

several rangers to drift off to sleep. As dawn nears, the patrol reestablishes radio contact. They learn air support will be available as soon as the fog blows off the mountain slope. It slowly grows lighter. The generator shuts off. Surely the enemy will come now. Everyone thinks it will be their last dawn.

By 0700 hours sounds of enemy movement intensify. Voices mingle with the barking of dogs. Waves of fear spread through the rangers. Tracker dogs! The NVA apparently have not yet pinpointed the rangers' position. Accompanied by the animals, enemy soldiers begin meticulously to fan out into the jungle to hunt their hidden foe.

The leader of Team Opel describes the situation to his commander over the radio. Gunship support is still at least an hour away. The commander recommends that the team blow its claymore mines and try to flee on the heels of the resultant devastation. In whispered conversation the team talks this plan over. One ranger feels "so damned scared," all he wants to do is "get the hell out of there." However, remembering the potential ambush sites seen when they hiked to their night position, the team decides to stay put. "Send help," they radio, "we are not going anywhere."

Enemy voices seem to be concentrated on three sides. The fourth side, toward the place where the helicopter had landed, appears clear. That cinches it. It is a trap. The NVA want the Americans to run in the seemingly safe direction. No doubt they have a major ambush set there. Team Opel hunkers down to wait some more.

A morning breeze clears the fog. Helicopter gunships finally arrive overhead. Just before 0900 hours the rangers see an enemy soldier carrying a rifle with a pistol at his belt running along a nearby trail. They direct the gunships toward this target. First come the sounds of the gunships, then the sound of rockets exploding, and last come the cries of wounded enemy soldiers.

Soon a second NVA appears. He comes within 20 meters of the patrol and raises his arm. One of the Americans sees a grenade in his hand. The ranger fires and the enemy soldier crumples to the ground. From the surrounding jungle a hail of enemy small-arms fire begins. Discovered at last, the Americans and their Kit Carson Scout fire back. Each ranger carries 25 to 30 clips of ammunition and eight grenades. The start of the firefight raises their spirits. After a harrowing night of waiting, being able to fire their weapons relaxes them. This was what they had been trained to do. It feels "good to know that we hadn't come here for nothing. If we were going to die we would make it expensive for the gooks," one ranger said later. They fight with confidence. But after an hour and a half their ammunition starts to run out. Two rangers have been hit by enemy grenades and are lightly wounded.

However, Team Opel knows help is on the way. An elite reaction team from the Air Cavalry, fondly known to the rangers as the "Blue Ghosts," is struggling through the jungle toward their position. Slowly enemy fire diminishes. A little later the Blue Ghosts arrive. "I could have kissed every one of them," recalls one ranger.

As Team Opel prepare to leave they gather their equipment including their eight claymore mines. They trace the 15-meter-long wires out from their positions to the claymores. Although most of the team had been awake all night, and at least two had been constantly vigilant, they find three wires have been cut. Two of their blasting caps have been stolen. A fourth mine has been turned around to face the ranger perimeter. If Team Opel had tried to blow the mines as advised, they would have killed their own men. The decision not to blow the mines had been a close call. They had chosen correctly.

Heading for the landing zone they spot a superbly camouflaged enemy bunker that they hadn't seen earlier. It is overlooking the route they had hiked along the evening before, sited at one of the places they had felt was particularly likely to feature an enemy ambush. From that vantage point the enemy had watched Team Opel enter the area.

If the NVA had been on to them from the start, why they hadn't attacked? the rangers speculated. Perhaps only a scout had manned the bunker. By the time he alerted his officers perhaps night had fallen and they couldn't quite locate the ranger position. Or perhaps the NVA feared that if they attacked, it would tip the Americans off to the presence of the base camp. The most intelligent deduction was that the NVA had tried to lure the rangers into a trap to kill them quickly before Team

Insignia of the "Blue Ghosts" —The call sign of Troop F, 8th Cavalry. An air cavalry troop, it provided aerial reconnaissance for the 23d Infantry Division and frequently worked with its long-range reconnaissance patrols.

Opel could radio for help. The rangers would never know for sure.

They did know that they had been up against "the best trained gooks we had ever fought." The NVA had exhibited good fire and movement tactics once the combat began, showing the practiced skill of veteran fighters.

The rangers had survived in a difficult situation. In war men create theories about why they live and others die. In Team Opel some reckoned it was partly due to their well-practiced sixth sense, the

Team Opel

BACK HOME: Weary, dishevelled but pleased to be back inside a US perimeter, men of a ranger team report for debriefing after being extracted from the combat zone by helicopter. A few hours rest, a shower and some beers, and they would be ready for another night mission.

ability to sense hidden danger. Others believed it was due to their Kit Carson Scout: "K.C. saved my life," several of them maintained. Or was survival partially due to the decision to stay put when their commander had recommended blowing the claymores and running? Or was it due to plain good luck?

The only certainty was that they had survived. The next day Ranger Team Opel went out on another long-range reconnaissance patrol to test that certainty again.

Learning to survive

IN THE MID-1960s, graduation from Fort Benning's
Ranger School placed a man a notch above the rest.
Ranger School was designed to tax a man's mental
and physical abilities to the utmost. If boot camp was
the grunt's college, Ranger School was where he
obtained a postgraduate education.

The Army's Field Manual published before
American ground troops went to war in Vietnam
spelled out how intense the ranger training was,
describing is as "realistic, rough, and to a degree,
hazardous. It is designed to develop the individual's
self-confidence, leadership, and skill." The training
sought to teach men to overcome mental and
physical obstacles. It began with rigorous physical
conditioning. Grueling individual and unit exercises, designed to condition the men to hardship
while getting them physically fit, continued
throughout the training period.

Aggressiveness was instilled through so-called
"combatives," drills involving hand-to-hand combat
and bayonet practice. Since rangers were expected
to operate behind enemy lines, special escape and
evasion (E & E) courses were featured. (When tried
in Vietnam, many of the E & E methods proved sad-
ly deficient.)

Confidence-building techniques were an important
feature of ranger training. The men were put
through a series of tests that seemed more difficult
than they actually were. They included a rope
drop—involving clambering over a cliff while supported by a rope and a suspension traverse—and
walking along a narrow rope suspended over a gorge
or river. These were the by-the-book conditioning
and confidence building exercises. In reality they
were supplemented by the imaginative whims and

fancies of the instructors, who came up with such tests as carrying a refrigerator up and down a hill repeatedly for 30 or 45 minutes.

Ranger School also taught survival skills. The soldiers learned how to survive in all types of terrain regardless of the weather. They learned how to live off the land, how to identify edible plants and animals, and how to construct shelters. A thorough understanding of map and compass work completed the survival aspects of the course.

Among the many other specialized skills taught at Ranger School were ambush techniques, cliff

Learning to survive

STATESIDE SIMULATOR: A Special Forces instructor stands guard at a specially re-created Viet Cong village at the Fort Bragg training center as American infantrymen dressed in the black pajamas of the Viet Cong reenact scenes likely to be encountered by US troops in South Vietnam. The array of National Liberation Front (NLF) Viet Cong flags are a reminder to trainee rangers that the enemy had grown so confident in some areas that they freely advertised their presence.

assault, and basic mountain climbing. But the heart of the program was patrolling. Soldiers practiced everything from the basics of caring for their weapons while operating in swamps to calling in artillery on map coordinates in a forest. Ranger School doctrine maintained that during patrols "hunger, fatigue, and tactical realism will uncover strengths and weakness that an individual does not know he possesses."

The Army hoped that the men who completed the tough Ranger School had absorbed the "Ranger Imprint," the ability and desire to conquer regardless

31

Training trap —A US soldier disguised as a member of the Viet Cong rolls back a mat at the entrance to the simulated Vietnamese village at the Fort Bragg training center to reveal a concealed punji trap. Here the trap, sharpened bamboo stakes pointing upwards, is guarded by a metal grid. In the real-life conditions of Vietnam, the pit would be covered by just a mat. Foot injuries to US troops from punji stakes led to the introduction of a new jungle boot with a steel-lined sole.

of the odds. By and large it worked. Ranger School graduates were soldiers who could think and act on their own under very trying circumstances.   In the years before the US sent ground forces to Vietnam, Army doctrine decreed that ranger skills should be spread throughout the military rather than concentrated in a few elite units. The Army deliberately resisted the temptation to create ranger units composed solely of Ranger School graduates. Instead it spread them around so that each infantry company could have at least one ranger-qualified officer and each platoon at least one ranger-qualified sergeant.

Individuals attended the Ranger School, received special training, and returned to their parent unit. When the war began, ranger-trained soldiers went into combat, but unlike previous wars, there were no separate ranger units.

Once American forces arrived in Vietnam, it quickly became apparent that finding the enemy would be a constant and major problem. This was to be grunt work: small infantry patrols sent out on regular searches to locate the Viet Cong and North Vietnamese forces. And the most hazardous type of patrol, without doubt, was the long-range reconnaissance patrol.

The concept of the long-range reconnaissance patrol (LRRP) derived from provisional recon companies that had been formed to support the Army in Germany in the early 1960s. In Vietnam the importance of intelligence gathering by infantry divisions gained further recognition and the system of having special attached recon units was continued and expanded. By 1967 each division had an LRRP company. Some units called themselves merely long-range patrols (LRP), but the two terms were interchangeable. The LRRP company, in turn, split up so each brigade had a recon detachment from which five- and six-man patrols were formed.

In the 9th Infantry Division, August 1967 marked the change from a platoon-sized recon unit to a full company LRRP outfit. Its elite unit became known as Company E, 50th Infantry. Where once LRRP platoons had trained at the Military Assistance Command, Vietnam (MACV) Recondo School, they were now put through a three-week course in long-range patrolling methods by the Green Berets, as the soldiers of the elite Special Forces were

known. The final exercise was an actual combat patrol.

The three-week school featured intensive exercises in map reading, navigation, intelligence, communication, supporting fire, emergency first aid, patrolling, and physical conditioning. Physical fitness was vital. Men had to be able to rapidly escape through rugged terrain once an LRRP unit broke contact. To prepare the LRRPs for this, instructors had the men build an obstacle course on which they practiced daily for the three weeks. The obstacle course supplemented forced road marches of up to seven miles in the morning and running in the afternoon. In spite of this rigorous conditioning, there were long waiting lists for LRRP training.

The main elements of an LRRP mission were usually reconnaissance, surveillance, target acquisition, and intelligence gathering. In practice, reconnaissance, or recon, meant scouting—moving through hostile territory to see what the enemy was up to. Surveillance usually involved setting up a camouflaged observation post overlooking a trail, bridge, or river crossing where enemy movement might be expected. Target acquisition followed from the first two duties.

Sometimes after the patrol had located the enemy it merely sat tight, recorded the information, and continued to watch. Other times the patrol helped

KNOW THINE ENEMY: An instructor shows a captured AK-47 rifle to students at a ranger school near An Khe operated by Company C of the 75th Ranger Battalion. Many rangers felt the rugged dependability of the AK-47 made it a superior weapon to the M-16.

Learning to survive

THE INSERTION:
A fully laden reconnaissance team moves away from a helicopter after being infiltrated into the MACV Recondo school site on Hon Long Island in the Bay of Nha Trang. Students spent three days on the island practicing techniques learned in the classroom. The final exercise at the school was an actual combat patrol beginning with a helicopter insertion.

outside forces "acquire" a target. They radioed news of the contact so that helicopter gunships, fixed-wing bombers, or artillery could bombard the unsuspecting enemy soldiers. The 101st Airborne's tactical instructions published in 1966 noted that by finding the enemy, LRRPs "enable the commander to employ troops and/or firepower in the most advantageous manner."

One of the highest-yielding forms of intelligence gathering was the "prisoner snatch." A patrol would ambush a small enemy force and try to capture a prisoner. It was not easy to overpower a man in these

circumstances without killing him. Even if the
patrol secured a live prisoner he would probably be
wounded. In any event the patrol then had to take
the prisoner to a clearing where a helicopter could
land to bundle him off. More commonly, intelligence
gathering meant rifling the pockets of dead enemy
soldiers to find documents that might reveal enemy
plans and intentions.

An LRRP mission began with an "insertion," a
helicopter landing of the patrol in a cleared area in
hostile territory. It was standard practice in most
units to fly the patrol leader over the landing

Insignia of the 1st Air Cavalry —Rich in helicopter resources, it developed the fast insertion tactic designed to conceal troop landings from a watching enemy.

zone (LZ) before the actual insertion so he could see the target area. Such quick helicopter overflights gave the leader a feel for the terrain and added a new perspective to the hours put in studying a map of the target area. Vietnam War era maps failed to reveal terribly important terrain details. Sometimes the helicopter recon filled them in.

The 1st Air Cav Division perfected helicopter insertion tactics. Rich in helicopter resources, it could afford to commit a three-flight lift team protected by two gunships for each insertion. Flying one behind another, the first lift helicopter carried the five- or six-man patrol, the second the commander, and the third remained empty, ready for any emergency. An obscure landing zone, often an old bomb crater or a small jungle clearing large enough to accommodate a single Huey lift ship, would be chosen for the insertion. The lead chopper dipped down, the patrol leaped off and headed for cover, the two following helicopters passed overhead, the lift Huey rose up becoming third in line, and the flight continued. This process required precise timing and skilled flying. It was designed to fool a watching enemy into thinking the flight had merely continued without interruption, thus hiding the fact that any men had been landed. Unless an observer happened to see the flight during the 5 to 10 seconds the lead Huey swooped to the ground, he would not realize anything unusual had occurred. Further concealment came from the fact that most insertions took place near dawn or dusk.

Once on the ground the team checked to determine if it had been observed, and then carefully proceeded to its first night defense position. A front scout led the way. Experienced in combat tracking, the front scout frequently paused to look and listen. He looked for signs of recently broken brush, human feces, or discarded rubbish. The best trackers could sometimes tell by smell or the warmth of the ground that the enemy had recently been in the area. The radioman traveled in the middle of the patrol. Depending on the standard operating procedure (SOP) of the unit the patrol served in, he made regular radio checks with headquarters. In the Air Cav these checks came twice a day, in the 25th Division officers demanded much more control and required frequent communications checks. In addition

Learning to survive

EVERYTHING THEY HAD:
Rangers on long-range reconnaissance patrols carried everything they needed into action. Laid out on this groundsheet (above) are one ranger's supplies, including submachine gun, ammunition clips, grenade launcher, grenades, four water bottles, C-rations, first-aid kit, water cleansing tablets, map, and compass. What a ranger could not carry, he improvised (below). At Recondo school a trainee strings together a crude antenna mast out of sticks.

Learning to survive

INSERTION DRILL: With the downrush from the propellers still sweeping their landing zone, rangers from a team at the Recondo school take up their positions. The rear scout's special responsibility is to watch for enemy tracker teams.

to the regular checks, the radioman reported enemy contacts. Special ground stations, "LRRP relays," dotted the countryside to receive and pass on radio messages from the patrols. Frequently an airborne communications relay plane flew overhead for the same purpose.

A rear scout walked last in line. His special responsibility was to watch the rear, frequently walking backwards to see if anyone followed the patrol. Everyone on the team understood that noise discipline was essential. Hand and arm signals were used extensively instead of voice commands. The team proceeded Indian-file, avoiding paths and

trails, preferring to "break bush," by striking off into the jungle parallel to existing trails.

After the first night, LRRPs adjusted their behavior to mimic the enemy. They moved when the enemy moved and slept when he slept. At least one team member remained on watch at all times. Even those not on alert didn't sleep soundly. They dozed or catnapped, waking up often to check the area around them. In each 24-hour period the patrol ate only once. The food was the dehydrated LRRP ration, a lighter, more sustaining meal than regular C-rations. The team had to carry enough food and water, supplemented by water purification tablets

Map reading —A ranger at Recondo school is shown how to make a quick map overlay. Intensive training in map reading was a key element in the education of a ranger. When it was overlooked disaster often followed.

if operating in areas of fresh water, to last on its own for five days. Theirs was a much different experience from that of the regular American combat soldier who demanded and received daily helicopter resupply of all the basics plus such creature comforts as cold beer, ice cream, and hot meals.

Most patrols followed no precise, preplanned route. This was left up to the team leader. Team leaders were specially selected sergeants. As combat losses took their toll, lower ranking specialist 4s began to lead patrols. Leaders had enormous responsibility, choosing when and where to move, and in the event of enemy contact whether to sit tight, attack, or flee.

A patrol never remained in the same place for consecutive nights, although the typical distance covered during a day of movement was a mere half kilometer. In the event the patrol made no contacts with the enemy, it traveled to the extraction point where again an elaborately orchestrated flying sequence occurred to bring a lift helicopter to just the right place at just the right moment. "Lurps," as the LRRP men were nicknamed, remember that moment well. "The best sight in the world is the sight of a chopper coming in for an extraction. Once you're aboard you feel like a kid who got a day off from school."

Even when a patrol failed to contact the enemy, the tension of remaining constantly alert and never knowing when a contact might occur physically and mentally drained the men. Standard procedures in the Air Cav Division recognized this. After a mission LRRP members were supposed to receive as much free time as possible during stand-down back at base. Yet in many cases, particularly in other divisions, a patrol no sooner completed one mission than it went out again. Such repeated patrolling reduced the men to a mind-numbed, zombie-like state. It contributed to some of the mutilation and atrocity incidents that were not uncommon among LRRPs/rangers.

All LRRPs were volunteers, usually aged 18 to 22 years, the age range for most infantry in Vietnam. Given the extreme danger and physical hardship of the long-range reconnaissance patrol, why did they volunteer? LRRPs attracted natural fighters: violent, aggressive young men who found satisfaction in the frequent, intensely personal, short-range fights that occurred on patrol. A few, like a soldier in the 9th Division who had served as a cannoneer with an artillery battery, volunteered when they "got bored and wanted a change." The patrols also appealed to free spirits: "In LRRPs you're more on your own, there's no rank pulling, I don't like army discipline and it works better here. It's army but not army, if you know what I mean."

Many more volunteered because they wanted the challenge of serving with the best. As one sergeant who had served in a regular infantry company before joining the LRRPs explained: "They are the best trained, and most closely integrated group of men found in the division." Addressing the lure of joining an elite unit, another veteran explained: "The men work as a team and feel a sense of team accomplishment unlike any other. Each man knows his job to perfection. Few men have more personal pride than a LRRP member. They enjoy going out. They are on their own. It is the pioneer-Indian spirit of besting their environment."

Once with a team, the men developed special bonds from shared experience and danger. "When you look at your buddy and he's scared, you know he feels the same way as you do and it helps." Veterans recognized that fear was natural and kept everyone alert. Controlling it was the key. One soldier who mastered his fear explained: "It's amazing how little you really worry when you're out there, it's more like being extra careful." The basic source of strength for any patrol came from mutual confidence and trust.

In a series of letters written from Vietnam to a friend, one soldier explained his motivations.

Field aid —A ranger corpsman learns how to give a shot to a fellow student at training school. Operating deep behind enemy lines and often without access to medevac helicopters, rangers had to learn how to take care of their own wounded.

I'm in a volunteer unit...we're called LRRPs, what we are is hunter-killer teams. Out in the field 4 days, 3 nights, then back at camp for 3-4 days.... [We have] the highest body count of all ranger companies in Nam... no friendly KIAs (killed in action) very few WIAs (wounded in action). God watches his LRRPs .... It's hard to find people to join 'cause people don't like working in small teams in the jungle.... with only 6 men it gets to ya, but I like it. I would hate to go to a line unit. All the noise would drive me nuts. Last time I

Learning to survive

INSERTION AND EXTRACTION: ''The best sight in the world is the sight of a chopper coming in for an extraction'' was a common sentiment among the rangers. Learning the fastest way in (left) and out (right) of a chopper was a prominent element in ranger training.

wrote I said I had 1 AK (Communist assault rifle) and would get another. . . . Well, next day our team went out and got three bodies and 3 AKs. So I got one. I've got 7 kills now. Usually I wouldn't tell anyone. Matter of fact you're the only one. But with your background and experience you'll understand. My wife, Mom and Dad think I recon areas for line units to set up. A safe job.

A confidential Army analysis published in 1968 noted the LRRPs received no extra pay or privileges for their work.

"Satisfaction comes from pride in their capabilities as a small, well trained, highly efficient unit. It also comes from the knowledge that most men shy away from their hazardous work."

The LRRPs in Vietnam were a fighting elite, and they knew it.

The buildup

The South Vietnamese rangers prepare for war

IN 1960 the American ambassador in Saigon read with alarm intelligence reports indicating that Communist guerrillas no longer operated in squads of 3 to 12 men but rather were attacking South Vietnamese installations in bands of up to 100 trained fighters. The ambassador's reports galvanized the Pentagon to send the Special Forces to South Vietnam to train the nation's soldiers. The Green Beret advisors recommended that ground forces receive a minimum training period of seven weeks. However, the desire to get troops on the field as quickly as possible overrode the Green Berets' advice. Combat instruction would last a mere four weeks, with South Vietnamese rangers attending some of the first courses.

At this time those in command of America's advisory force did not see a Vietnamese ranger project as an asset and suggested the project could be phased out. They worried that it over-concentrated scarce resources into one project. But the South Vietnamese president, the then-powerful Ngo Dinh Diem, saw the formation of ranger units as a way to protect his increasingly unpopular rule. Although American advisors didn't favor the existence of ranger units in the first place, they believed that if ranger-trained soldiers were available they should be spread throughout the Army rather than concentrated in elite units. Ignoring this advice, the South Vietnamese general staff unanimously endorsed the decision to add recon (the Americans called them ranger) companies to the regular Army. Each Army of the Republic of South Vietnam (ARVN) division was to have three such companies.

In time the ARVN rangers became skilled fighting troops. But at first the ranger program fell prey to

Insignia of the Special Forces

Ngo Dinh Diem —President of South Vietnam, 1954-63. He declined to follow US practice and instead of dispersing rangers among regular army units, he kept them together as potentially elite units. Diem, who had no popular power base, hoped the new ranger units would stay loyal to him. But none came to his rescue in the coup of 1963 when he was executed by a junior officer.

inefficiency and corruption. When the first ranger class received top priority, 218 out of 311 officers and men graduated. In the second class and out of the limelight, 63 students withdrew within the first two weeks. Thereafter desertion, malingering, disease, and myriad other problems continued to undermine the training effort. Although the rangers were supposed to spearhead the fight against the Viet Cong, orders and directives governing the formation of the ranger force were ignored. The 9,000-man ranger force became a special branch of the Army, but they were elite in name only. Their performance did not justify that prestigious title.

South Vietnam's Ranger Training Center was established in 1961. It featured jungle, swamp, and mountain schools taught by American specialists. The center tried to toughen up the students for a war that was becoming increasingly bitter. Slowly the quality of ranger units improved, in part due to this training and in part because the ranger battalions were the only ARVN forces allowed to participate in refresher courses on a regular basis. By 1965, as American ground forces entered the war, ranger units comprised over one-fifth of the total number of ARVN infantry battalions.

The continued rapid expansion of the South Vietnamese military saw a corresponding decline in unit quality. An American study in 1967, focusing on one of the four tactical zones in South Vietnam, singled out two ranger battalions as having ineffective leadership and poor combat ability. Clearly some ranger battalions remained elite only in name. Only when the head of the American forces in Vietnam, General William Westmoreland, threatened to withhold military assistance from these units did their performance improve.

Viewing this discouraging situation, an American officer reported: "While there are many outstanding exceptions, surprisingly large numbers of this officer corps seemed to lack aggressiveness, leadership ability, and a full professional commitment." He noted that many officers preferred rear-area assignments rather than combat commands and many seemed "to use their positions for personal or even financial advantage."

By the time American ground forces withdrew from the war, there were 37 ranger border defense

The buildup

BACK TO SCHOOL:
A US Army advisor coaches a South Vietnamese ranger in the use of a submachine gun at the Ranger School in 1962. The early 1960s saw a steady buildup of US advisors to Vietnam. By 1964 there were 16,000 US personnel in South Vietnam instructing the Vietnamese in every aspect of modern warfare. Many advisors went on missions with the newly trained ARVN rangers but because they did not have combat status they could only fire at the enemy when fired upon.

47

Gen. William C. Westmoreland —US commander in Vietnam, 1964-68. On several occasions he threatened to withhold funds from ARVN ranger battalions because of their autocratic treatment of civilians—often forcing them to hand over food at gunpoint. Loss of cooperation among the civilian population hindered intelligence-gathering operations.

battalions and 21 regular ranger battalions compared to about 120 line infantry units. But the dilution in quality caused by the tremendous expansion in size remained quite evident. The ranger border defense battalions had formerly been militia units. Again, merely renaming them did nothing to improve their combat ability. By and large the 21 regular ranger battalions had become top-notch units. Along with the ARVN airborne and Marine units, they acted as "fire brigade troops," rushing to contain VC/NVA breakthroughs, and spearheading South Vietnamese counterstrokes.

Although of uneven quality from top to bottom, a well-trained, well-led ARVN ranger unit could and did perform remarkable acts of courage and bravery.

In the summer of 1967 combat all over Vietnam intensified. During the previous year a labyrinth of ports, airfields, depots, and bases had been built to support American combat operations. The year 1967 would be the year the American military took to the field in a big way. Most South Vietnamese forces were to be involved in an important, yet secondary role. While American forces sought out and engaged the enemy main force, ARVN units would perform so-called "pacification" missions, bringing the hamlets and villages under ARVN control. The ARVN rangers were an exception to this plan. Their ranks included many of the best fighters in the South Vietnamese military. Pacification was not for them. They were aggressive. Like the Americans, they would find and fight the tough VC/NVA regular units.

The ARVN ranger role had changed considerably since ranger units had first been conceived. Originally organized for LRRP-type operations, the ARVN companies were designed to operate independently during scouting and raider missions. Their light equipment relected this intent. By 1967 ranger companies acted together in battalion-sized conventional operations, but still with the same equipment. Consequently they lacked staying power for sustained combat.

When Captain Keith Nightingale became the senior advisor to the 52d ARVN Rangers, one of the first things he did was use his American military contacts to scrounge equipment. Procurement through regular channels simply didn't work. The

advisor's unofficial job was to step out of the chain of command to find weapons, ammunition, food, and housing for the families of ARVN rangers. The importance of this last element could not be overlooked. No soldier could be expected to lay his life on the line for a cause that failed to provide his family with the necessities for life. It was a never-ending battle for an advisor to overcome official corruption to obtain these necessities. Improving the standard of living of the rangers' families paid direct dividends. When Nightingale was able to provide lumber, metal, and canvas for 225 family dwellings, he knew he had just increased the combat power of 225 field soldiers.

Another factor that had impaired the 52d's combat efficiency and lowered the soldiers' morale was more conventional. It was a matter of firepower; the rangers had been outgunned when fighting both NVA regulars and main force VC units. Their light carbines were no match for the Communist AK-47 assault rifle. To compensate, Nightingale helped the rangers secure M-16 rifles. He procured eleven M-60 and nine .50-caliber machine guns to replace the much lighter, standard issue .30-caliber machine guns. He located one 4.2-inch and three 81mm mortars to substitute for the standard 60mm mortars. Upgunning the rangers allowed them to fight on

RIFLE CHECK:
The commander of an ARVN ranger battalion inspects a radio operator's M-16 for cleanliness. It was not until 1969 and the introduction of Nixon's Vietnamization policy that ARVN forces were equipped with the more powerful M-16 automatic. During the action at Suoi Long the M-16 allowed the 52d Rangers to compete on equal terms.

49

The buildup

LIFELINE:
A US advisor instructs men from the 2d ARVN Ranger Pathfinders on the use of the PRC-25 radio. Capable of being carried by one man, the transistorized FM receiver-transmitter provided 920 channels for two-way communications at company and platoon level. Its size, scope, range, and reliability revolutionized field communication. Many rangers considered the PRC-25s to be "worth their weight in gold."

equal terms with the enemy. Even more important were the scrounged radios. The table of organization called for equipping the 52d with only a few short-range radios. By calling upon cooperative American units and occasionally dipping into the black market, the captain helped the ARVN rangers obtain 10 of the much better PRC-25 radios. Recognizing that "good radios made the difference between life and death," the American advisor felt that the PRC-25s were "worth their weight in gold."

With an authorized strength of 658 men, the battalion, usually understrength, entered the field with

450 soldiers organized into four companies and a
headquarters detachment. The radios let them stay
in touch as they dispersed across rugged terrain.
Generally the 52d moved in two parallel columns
400 meters apart. This distance was finely
calculated to be far enough apart so a single ambush
could not hit both columns, but close enough
together for mutual protection. The all-important
radio link gave the ranger commander the ability
to manipulate the two maneuver/reaction columns.

Experience had shown that merely having the
right equipment did not make for a good fighting

Hurried inspection —Gen. Earle G. Wheeler inspects training facilities at a ranger training center at Duc My in 1963. At this stage most ARVN ranger units were considered elite in name only. Just turning peasants into soldiers was considered an achievement by the US advisors who trained them.

force. A unit also needed good personnel and good leadership. The 52d Ranger Battalion had both. Its men were all volunteers. They received better training than regular ARVN infantry units, including a stint at the South Vietnamese Ranger Training Center. The men also received proficiency pay that exceeded the normal pay scale. Although the rangers had trouble getting along with their own civilian countrymen, they were considered by the Americans to be good, aggressive soldiers who liked to kill VC.

For leadership the 52d looked to Major Hiep, a graduate of Vietnam's prestigious Dalat Military Academy. Hiep had served in the armed forces since 1952 when he fought with the French Colonial Army. He had earned France's highest honor for bravery, the Croix de Guerre, and held all South Vietnam's valor awards including the equivalent of the Medal of Honor. He was the type of leader an American advisor respected and could get along with. All in all the 52d Rangers was an elite unit. It would need every advantage in its next operation.

At 1400 hours the afternoon of 27 June 1967, helicopters landed Hiep and some 260 rangers in a flat cleared area near Suoi Long. The field lay baking in the 90-degree heat. Numerous trails emerged from the surrounding secondary jungle. Hiep formed his men into two columns and set off. Intelligence believed that an enemy company-sized base camp was nearby. Intelligence had provided a VC deserter (the official term for these men was "rallier" since they had rallied to the Allied cause) who was to lead the 52d to the base. After moving about 900 meters through the steamy underbrush, the rallier told Hiep that they were getting close.

The first contact came at 1600 hours. Hiep deployed his men and ordered an assault. The VC position was a "typical base camp, you couldn't see it till you were on top of it." It featured interlocking trenches and bunkers with overlapping fields of fire. Three bunkers guarded the camp from the direction of the ranger assault. Each had a firing slot only one foot above ground with four feet of overhead cover and housed a 12.67mm Chicom machine gun.

The 52d's initial attack took the defenders by surprise. The rangers captured about one-third of the enemy perimeter, killed the VC battalion

The buildup

UNCOVERED:
An ARVN ranger in "duck hunter" combat fatigues inspects a Viet Cong trenchline and machine gun bunker uncovered during a three-day sweep of the notorious Iron Triangle, a VC stronghold close to Saigon. Machine gun bunkers and shallow "spider holes"—sufficient to house a sniper—were sited to provide overlapping fields of fire. With dirt roofs often several feet thick, they could only be penetrated by direct hits from grenades or by air attacks.

The buildup

commander, and captured several mortars. Long-range 175mm American artillery pieces, capable of firing 20 miles, supported the attack. However a short round that nearly annihilated the lead ranger platoon forced Nightingale to call off these guns. More artillery support was lost when an ARVN battery ceased fire after a short bombardment because it had used up its day's allotment of ammunition.

Undaunted, Major Hiep ordered his rangers to hold their position and prepare for an enemy counterattack. He thought the VC would try to recapture the weapons and supplies they had lost

in the rangers' first rush. Hiep also requested ARVN reinforcements, but his request was turned down. His four companies would fight alone, backed by only one small militia unit.

The base backed on a river. Shortly after dusk a thick fog rose from the water. The fog concealed several barges which began to ferry enemy reinforcements from the far shore. Later the rangers learned that some two and a half battalions of enemy soldiers had crossed the water to reinforce the base camp. Alert ranger scouts detected the VC movement, but in the fog they failed to recognize the size

Captured —ARVN rangers surround a Viet Cong prisoner of war. The Vietnamese on both sides had little time for the niceties of war and US commanders had to emphasize to their ARVN counterparts the intelligence and propaganda gains to be had from treating prisoners humanely.

of the enemy's buildup. However, three times the scouts saw something surprising: five broadchested and hairy Caucasians moving amidst an enemy command group. Later the rangers figured they were Russian advisors, present to administer what they must have thought would be the rangers' coup de grace.

Close to dawn, 0530 hours, Hiep issued orders for his men to assault the enemy camp. He didn't know that 1,500 enemy soldiers simultaneously received orders to attack the rangers. Each of Hiep's companies held a 75- to 100-meter front. Hordes of VC swept toward their positions in a massed, human wave assault. Forty meters behind the first wave came another company-sized line of charging enemy soldiers. Forty meters further back a third wave filled the trenches as they too prepared to attack. Soon the 52d was fighting for its life.

Just in time help arrived. At 0615 hours, helicopter gunships appeared. Their rockets and machine guns wiped out the lead VC company. According to Nightingale, "they took them out from one end to another." Emboldened by the destruction of the first assault wave, Hiep ordered the rangers to attack again. It proved impossible. Outnumbered six or seven to one, the 52d went over to the defensive.

The VC attacked again under cover of a blistering mortar bombardment. The American advisor got lucky. He heard the mortar bombs falling into their tubes before they fired. He got a compass bearing and radioed an azimuth to the L-19 observation plane. The pilot rocketed the target, destroying the mortars.

Although reinforcements were coming, Hiep realized he had to withdraw or face total destruction. To cover the retreat he ordered his second company to assault. Under cover of this assault most of the 52d staggered to the rear. The second company was nearly annihilated in the sacrificial attack.

Soon the VC reorganized and again pressed the attack. By hugging right up against the ranger position, the enemy tried to avoid Allied bombs and shells. The rangers marked their forward position with smoke grenades. Ten seconds later American B-57 bombers blasted the smoke with 1,000-pound time-delay bombs. In this way Allied firepower

defeated the VCs' "hugging tactics." Although over 300 VC were killed by the devastating bombardment, two ranger platoons were also virtually wiped out when they failed to get far enough away from the deadly aerial onslaught. The surviving rangers fell back by bounds and dug in.

Around 1000 hours another ARVN ranger unit arrived to relieve the 52d. As Hiep and Nightingale moved around their defensive perimeter they estimated losses at 40 killed, 100 wounded, and close to 100 missing. Of the 260 rangers who began the mission, they could find only 36 unwounded survivors.

Allied reinforcements swept into the base camp that afternoon. A VC blocking force skillfully covered the enemy's retreat using captured claymore mines, snipers, and small ambushes. The next day the American 11th Armored Cavalry arrived to "walk all over the camp." For two more days the 52d patrolled the area finding groups of two and three rangers who had been shaken loose from their units during the overwhelming enemy assault and

MORTAR FIRE: M-113 armored personnel carriers from the 11th Armored Cavalry fire on an enemy position prior to a mobile assault. After the battle of Suoi Long, M-113s from the 11th swept the area in a mobile attack, mopping up pockets of enemy resistance.

The buildup

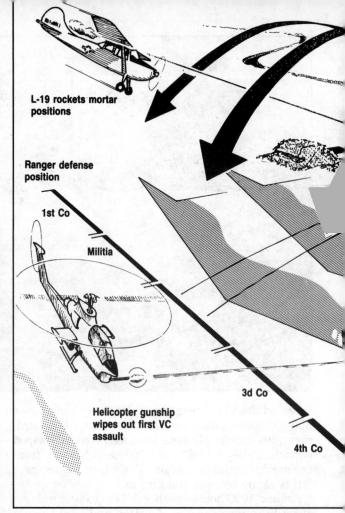

L-19 rockets mortar positions

Ranger defense position

1st Co

Militia

3d Co

Helicopter gunship wipes out first VC assault

4th Co

BATTLE OF SUOI LONG: This map shows how the 52d ARVN Rangers earned a unit citation for overcoming superior odds in the four-day battle of Suoi Long. Driven back after a first attack when they captured some enemy mortars, they faced successive waves of Viet Cong attacks. The first was destroyed by helicopter gunship fire and the second by fire from an L-19 spotter plane directed on target by a US advisor.

had hidden in the jungle until they found friendly soldiers. These survivors reduced the casualty list to 28 killed, 82 wounded, and 12 missing: a casualty rate of close to 50 percent.

Three days after the fight, the 52d found a ranger sergeant from the second company, the unit that had made the sacrificial covering assault. The sergeant had walked 15 kilometers carrying a wounded buddy. As he carried this load he supported another ranger who was hobbled by a leg wound. The sergeant reported seeing a large concentration of enemy soldiers at a certain location. The American high command ordered a B-52 strike to hit this spot. US intelligence later claimed that the giant bombers

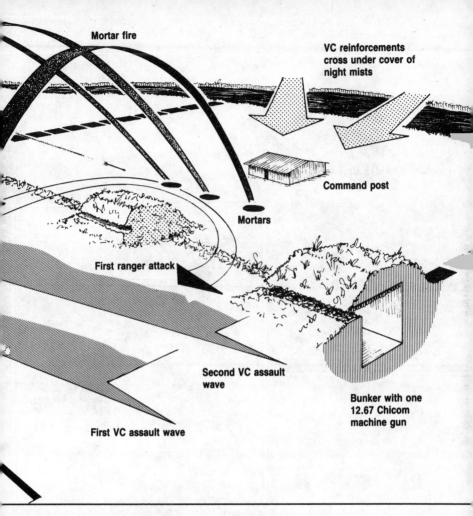

Mortar fire

VC reinforcements
cross under cover of
night mists

Command post

Mortars

First ranger attack

Second VC assault
wave

Bunker with one
12.67 Chicom
machine gun

First VC assault wave

had struck the enemy headquarters for all military operations in South Vietnam, the so-called Central Office for South Vietnam (COSVN) base camp, killing the overall commander of VC/NVA forces in South Vietnam. Sources in Hanoi, the North Vietnamese capital, would later claim that the commander had died of cancer.

The four-day operation at Suoi Long earned the 52d Rangers a Vietnamese Presidential Unit Citation. For six months their opponents remained inactive, licking their wounds. Under Major Hiep's aggressive leadership, the 52d had justified their special training and equipment that made the rangers an ARVN elite.

Nam's Angels

4

The trailblazers of War Zone C

THE ROAR of souped-up motorcycles split the air. The reconnaissance patrol of the 3d Battalion, 22d Infantry, 25th Division, was returning to camp. First came four outriders wearing flak jackets and crash helmets and riding Honda 175cc motorcycles. Following their lead were two specially equipped jeeps carrying machine guns. Last in line was a three-quarter-ton truck armed with a .50-caliber weapon. Standing at the camp gate, the CBS reporter could barely contain his excitement. Here was a story if ever he had seen one. The unit looked like they belonged in a Hollywood movie. It seemed like Hell's Angels, the Rat Patrol, and the Wild Ones all wrapped into one. The reporter motioned with his arm toward the vehicles. In a cloud of dust the patrol zoomed by. The reporter jumped up and down, waving his arms, trying to attract the patrol's attention.

Lieutenant Steve Campbell sat in his command jeep. Glancing to his side he saw someone acting weird. "I wonder what that idiot wants?" he thought. He didn't care. The day's mission was over and Campbell had thoughts only for the drinks waiting back at his hootch. Leaving the CBS man in the dust by the roadside, the 25th Division's long-range reconnaissance patrol sped on.

The persistent reporter decided he would have to find out who these guys were. In a most unconventional war, here was a peculiar unit by any standards. He tracked Campbell down that night and learned some of the story behind the motorized unit. It began in June 1968, in War Zone C, three kilometers from the Cambodian border.

Campbell had led his 10-man LRRP team into their night ambush position. They set the eight

TRAILBLAZERS:
Four of the original ten Nam's Angels (left to right): Dennis Verbrigghie, Jim Linder, Scott Anderson, and Jim Tomusco.

claymore mines to sweep a hardpacked trail that ran through the triple canopy jungle. Then they waited. Around 2200 hours a distant sound disrupted the normal noise of the jungle at night.

"What's that?" whispered a soldier to the lieutenant.

"I don't know," he replied.

"Sounds like a chain saw," someone hissed.

"Yeah, what the hell's that for?"

"Shit, they're sawing wood."

"Maybe the gooks are building bunkers."

"Holy shit, that's it. We're in the middle of a VC bunker complex. They're building bunkers all around us!"

The team was getting a little bit panicky. Over-active imaginations had taken an unrecognizable sound and turned it into an image of a Viet Cong base camp full of soldiers itching to kill rangers. The 20-year-old Campbell was plenty scared himself, but he calmed his men: "Let's just wait and listen." In

Going down under —An instructor at Ranger School demonstrates a fast descent from a 55-foot tower using a technique known as the "Australian Rappel." It was one of several techniques designed to build up a ranger's self-confidence.

a few minutes the noise grew louder. One team member, SP4 James Linder of Indianapolis, Indiana, spoke up: "Lieutenant, it's one of those damn gook mopeds." Everyone in the LRRP team knew Linder spoke with authority. Linder had grown up near the famed Indianapolis speedway and had raced motorcycles professionally before coming to Vietnam.

Campbell passed the word around: "We got us a courier coming this way. Be quiet, let him into the kill zone, and we'll nail him."

Not knowing what might be following the moped, Campbell decided to blow half his claymores and save the rest for whatever else came along. He preferred using the claymores and grenades in an ambush. They were reliable and didn't miss.

The engine sound increased. The men could make out a dim headlight coming along the trail. The unsuspecting rider entered the kill zone. Four explosions shattered the night air as the team detonated the mines. Campbell popped a small trip flare and held it. By its light the team examined the scene. The bloody, riddled body of the rider had been blown off the trail. Next to him was an AK-47 and the dented wreckage of his moped. A Chinese flashlight was strapped to the handlebars to act as a headlight. Wire from a US-manufactured claymore mine secured the flashlight onto the bike.

Campbell hurriedly searched the corpse, removing some grenades and a parcel of documents. Worried about what might be coming along the trail he said, "Let's move out."

Linder, the ex-professional motorcycle racer, had been eyeing the moped covetously. "Lieutenant, let me take this along, I want to tinker with it."

Sergeant Scott Anderson chimed in, "Yeah, I'll help carry it!"

Thinking they must be joking, Campbell looked at them closely. He knew his men. They were serious.

"Okay. Look you sons of bitches, you can have it if you keep up 'cause we're not getting into a firefight over some crazy piece of junk."

Campbell was a ranger. Part of his ranger training stressed the importance of having an escape plan worked out before actually engaging the enemy. His veteran team knew the plan. They would run 300 yards along the trail, head into an extremely thick

bamboo grove to throw off pursuit, cross a small stream, and wait by a clearing where a helicopter could extract them at first light. The team set off at a jog, Linder and Anderson half carrying, half dragging the moped along the ground.

They arrived at the LZ with lungs aching and hearts pumping. They had no idea if the enemy was following. The patrol waited for dawn to come and the rescue chopper to appear. The helicopter pilots were used to picking up rangers. Normally they would not bother to land, but would just hover while the rangers sprinted to the chopper and climbed on. The pilots knew that the rangers were often hard-pressed when calling for extraction. Under such circumstance neither party wanted to waste any time.

Dawn arrived and the lead Huey gunship flew into the clearing checking for the enemy. It signalled "all clear" and the pickup bird arrived. The rangers walked toward it, Linder and Anderson carrying the moped. The helicopter hovered in the clearing. Campbell saw the pilot look out, nudge the co-pilot, point toward the men hauling the moped, drop his jaw in amazement, and set the chopper onto the ground with a thump.

There wasn't alot of room inside. The team packed aboard with the moped in the middle. The heavily

GRENADE GALLERY: A cross-section of the types of grenades used by the Viet Cong and kept on display at Ranger School so that students could identify enemy weapons. The stick grenades were all homemade, the pineapple and smooth grenades were copied from Chicom and Soviet designs. The Zippo lighter and cigarette pack are for size reference.

65

ANGEL PATROL: Two Angels lead a patrol outside FSB Washington, northeast of Tay Ninh City, in May 1969. The motorcyclists in the squad presented hard-to-hit targets.

loaded chopper took off. The pilot yelled back to Campbell: "What's that?"

"Great booty," replied the pleased Lieutenant, "better than an AK-47, or even that battle flag we got last time. No one's ever brought back a cycle."

By the time the helicopter returned to Tay Ninh base, the rangers had made their plan. Lieutenant Colonel Carmichael met them as they disembarked. "What the hell you got there?"

Campbell explained what had happened on the mission and then hatched the next part of his team's plot: "We're going to get drunk, set up an obstacle

course, and you are going to be the first to drive the cycle through it."

"I don't know about that" said the colonel, "but I'll come watch."

Linder successfully got the moped running in time for the big event. The rangers built an obstacle course using full beer cans to mark the slalom gates. The contest involved elapsed time and how many cans the rider picked up along the way. The "base warriors" from the nearby bars and lounges attended the contest. The ex-pro from Indianapolis won easily and everyone retired to celebrate with

Wet rat
—A ranger
student is
hauled out of
the water after a
mishap on a
patrolling
exercise.
Images of "Rat
Patrol" style
glory were
dispelled by the
realities of
ranger training.

the beer. That night the rangers got drunk and planned the next step in their campaign.

When Colonel Carmichael visited the following day, the rangers were ready. Describing the successful ambush, Campbell put forward a proposition: "You know, if we had real trail bikes we could really get some things done." The ranger's normal area of operation covered rubber plantations and jungles full of hard packed, so-called "high-speed" trails used by the Viet Cong to transport supplies and equipment from Cambodia into the interior of Vietnam. A motorized unit could operate on these trails covering much more ground than a foot patrol.

"I don't know," replied the skeptical colonel.

Campbell tried a different approach: "We could get some jeeps, mount heavy weapons on them, and be just like the Rat Patrol." This struck a responsive chord. *The Rat Patrol* was then a popular TV program chronicling the exploits of a motorized unit in World War II that had fought the Germans in North Africa. Here was an idea an Army career officer could understand. The colonel promised to test the idea further up the chain of command.

Sometime later, Campbell got word to visit the brigade's motor pool. His men in tow, the lieutenant arrived to see four brand-new showroom stock street bikes, fresh out of their packing crates.

"Isn't this a typical army 'fubar' (fucked up beyond all recognition)," said a disgusted Specialist Linder. All the rangers laughed. While back in the States one could easily outfit a "trail bike" with special features for cross-country performance, the Army's cycle, equipped with a regular engine and smooth street tires, would have a tough time out in the field.

Linder examined the cycles and thought awhile. "What the hell," he pronounced. "Let's try it."

The only modifications to the cycles were the addition of a skid plate, saddle bags, squad radio, and a CAR-15 automatic rifle mounted with a swivel on the handlebars. Two jeeps and a three-quarter-ton truck completed the unit.

When the unit was ready Campbell went to the colonel and reported. He planned to take a patrol to Mo Cong, a village 40 miles away deep in VC territory. In the past the rangers had used the village as a staging area after being inserted by helicopters. This time Campbell proposed they drive to the

Nam's Angels

TOP BIKE:
Lt. Steve Campbell, the unit's creator and leader, at FSB Buell in April 1969. In August Campbell's rangers put aside their bikes to fight conventionally to help repel a heavy NVA attack against the fire support base.

Nam's Angels

AMBUSH: Moments before this photograph was taken the motorcyclists had surprised six Viet Cong setting up a rocket launcher in a clearing to the right. Both of the unit's jeeps had been fitted with M-60 machine guns which were quickly turned on the VC. To maintain a rapid rate of fire a sergeant (left) acts as the loader, feeding the ammunition belt. The motorcycle rangers were frequently used as bait to draw the enemy. When this happened Campbell adopted shoot-and-scoot tactics, with the bikers getting out at top speed while the jeeps provided covering fire.

village: "I want to show Charlie we've got something new on the block."

"It could be dangerous," said the colonel.

"We've got to try," replied Campbell.

The lieutenant was not heedless of the risks involved. To help even the odds he carefully arranged for artillery support to cover the entire trip. He particularly alerted the artillery to the map coordinates where he felt the greatest risk of ambush lay. But mostly the ranger relied upon surprise. He was certain the Viet Cong had never seen anything like his motorized rangers.

The trip went uneventfully. When they arrived at Mo Cong the regional forces (RFs, or Ruff Puffs) couldn't believe what they saw. The cyclists roared into the village center, stopped, and revved their engines for effect. The jeeps and truck arrived and the place went crazy. It was as if they had been liberated. The villagers and Ruff Puffs alike cheered and crowded around the cycles. The rangers unloaded cartons of C rations to give the villagers. They in turn asked to touch the cycles, to sit on them, start the engines, have their pictures taken next to the vehicles. It reminded Campbell of a film

Not all glamor —Under the unsympathetic gaze of an instructor a student at Ranger School performs extra calisthenics for making a mistake during a rappelling exercise.

he had seen of the liberation of France in World War II.

After an overnight stay the rangers prepared to leave. "We'll be back," Campbell promised.

"When?" asked the officer in charge of the Ruff Puffs.

Mindful of the high probability that this officer worked both sides—there was no way an outpost like his could survive unless it had made some accommodation with the enemy—the ranger answered: "You'll see."

"You're afraid we will ambush you and take the cycles," said the officer with a smile.

Campbell smiled back, but that was exactly what he feared.

In the ensuing weeks the motorized rangers were deployed to find fresh trail activity, locate safe landing zones, and conduct fast road sweeps for convoy operation. One month after the trip to Mo Cong the CBS reporter encountered them returning from patrol and Nam's Angels were on their way to national attention. The reporter and a film crew accompanied the unit on a four-day patrol. His report brought flocks of other reporters to Tay Ninh to see this crazy, gung-ho ranger unit. Newspapers in the States picked the story up. *Time* magazine gave it coverage.

The press reported that the battalion commander believed that the unit's unique mobility was well suited for the maze of trails that cut through War Zone C. It quoted the battalion's executive officer as saying: "At first I was very leery of the whole idea, but now I am confident it was a good one. Recon has provided us with valuable information which normally we would not have."

Campbell's mother read about the creation of a motorized unit: "That's just like my son," she thought. In high school he had always been known as an inventor and organizer. Two years earlier he formed his high school's first powder puff football team, its first frat, and its first underground newspaper. Nam's Angels was just more of the same, thought Mrs. Campbell.

Other people in the States also read about the unit. A letter arrived from a branch of the motorcycle gang known as Hell's Angels. They volunteered to come over and help their brothers. The rangers got

a big laugh from that one. Even better was a letter written to President Johnson by an Atlanta, Georgia, cycle buff. The letter worked its way along channels until it arrived in Tay Ninh. Opening it in his hooch, Campbell read the earnest writer's critique of the Honda 175cc cycle. The letter concluded: "Watch out! It will lock up at the worst moments." The rangers, who were fabricating parts off the black market to keep the machines running, were immensely amused.

While popular acclaim through the press and acceptance by their own officers were gratifying, nothing surpassed the effect the unit had on certain important people in Tay Ninh City. The civilians called them "Motorcycle Soldiers" and always gave them special attention. In particular, the madam of their favorite bar/brothel looked out for them. She encouraged the rangers to bring their cycles right into her bar and park them on the dance-room floor. Bringing out a bottle of vintage French cognac, she poured Campbell a glass and toasted him: "You are very special aren't you?" The 20-year-old ranger felt obliged to agree.

That night she "souvenired" everyone. The drinks and the girls were on the house. The rangers found that the shiny cycles had the same effect on teenage Vietnamese girls as they had had on girls back in

Nam's Angels

RECON BY FIRE: After suspicious movement had been spotted in a nearby woodline, a machine gunner tries recon by fire—firing at random to try to flush out the enemy. Mounted on the unit's three-quarter-ton truck, the M2 .50-caliber machine gun was the Angels's heaviest weapon. Standing on the tailboard is a forward artillery observer whose role was to call artillery and air support by radio.

the States. "They got hot when they saw them," recalls one of Nam's Angels. As the party continued, one particularly attractive girl fondled Linder's bike. After undressing and rubbing up against the seat like a cat, she stood and pointed at the owner: "That's for you."

The 200-pound former cycle pro rose shakily—the whisky was taking its toll—and roared: "Nobody touches that bike but me."

"Hey Linder," replied one of his comrades, "I'll give you a month's pay just to smell the seat."

"It ain't even worth six months' pay, 'cause you,

my good buddy, might be dead come tomorrow."

Brief crazy moments like these overshadowed by the knowledge that sudden death could hit at any time were the reality of Vietnam for young, adventuresome Americans who joined the rangers.

In the ensuing months Nam's Angels proved adept at uncovering mortar and rocket sites. While enemy light infantry on foot could easily evade the noisy patrol, they could not move their heavy equipment before the fast-moving rangers arrived. The men enjoyed their motorized operations. One bike rider, SP4 James Tomusco, explained: "It sure beat walking

Hidden hazard —A sergeant probes gently around a VC mine buried along a trail. The mine that caused the most damage to vehicles was the 23-pound Chicom mine. Its pressure-operated detonator required the weight of a vehicle to make it explode.

in the sun on a hot day." However, they felt restricted by their cycles' poor cross-country performance: "If we had a Harley motor in a frame like this we'd really have something," claimed one ranger. The four riders wanted a tough, powerful dirt bike "with big drive sprockets, knobby wheels, and more vroom."

The 25th Division adapted to the novel situation of having a motorized ranger unit. Its commanders developed new tactics. Lieutenant Campbell began to realize that in spite of the briefings that explained his mission with such terms as "fast recon to investigate trail activity," what his men were really being asked to do was to act as bait. They were being sent into enemy-controlled areas with the expectation that the Viet Cong would hit them. When this happened the division's regular infantry and artillery units would have a target to strike using even greater force.

Accordingly, Campbell devised his own new tactics. He called them "shoot and scoot." When the enemy opened fire on his cyclists, the bikers would get out at high speed while the machine-gun-mounted jeeps and truck provided covering fire with their M-60s and .50-cal weapons. With that the rangers had done their job. They had drawn the enemy's fire and disengaged. Campbell would radio a report of the contact back to base and leave it up to the higher command as to what to do next.

Inevitably Nam's Angels lost men. One day an enemy ambush allowed the motorcycles and jeeps to pass through the kill zone. A mine then demolished the truck, killing two and badly wounding three rangers. The jeeps and cyclists returned to the truck to provide protection while a medevac helicopter was called. This was the worst single blow to hit Nam's Angels. None of the four cycle riders was ever touched by enemy fire. Amazingly, four rangers acting as motorcycle scouts rode through enemy-infested jungle terrain for over a year without loss.

Nam's Angels believed their special mobility kept them from getting hit. A fast-moving target that appeared suddenly from an unexpected direction was a hard target to shoot at. Years later in 1981, the Army assigned the 9th Infantry Division the task code-named High Technology Test Bed to test all

Nam's Angels

PROPAGANDA COUP: An ARVN ranger examines the remains of boxes of Viet Cong propaganda captured during a lightning raid. Often, as the men of the 101st discovered during their 12-minute raid, it was the surprise attacks that paid the best dividends.

Nam's Angels

THE PRICE: Nam's Angels leader Lt. Steve Campbell with the unit's three-quarter-ton truck wrecked by an antitank mine. Two of his rangers died and three were wounded during this August 1969 incident on a trail into Mo Cong village.

sorts of equipment to provide extra mobility to American fighting men. The veterans of Nam's Angels felt compelled to write to the division's commanding general to advise him of their experiences. The ex-rangers believed they had proven a thing or two about mobile tactics out on the jungle trails of War Zone C.

Nam's Angels was not a typical unit. Indeed, even the men who belonged to the 25th Division's recon platoon spent much of the time performing more conventional long-range patrol, ambush, and prisoner snatch missions. Throughout Vietnam the LRRP/ranger mission usually involved an extended three- to five-day operation deep in enemy territory. But LRRPs were nothing if not versatile, and were thus able to perform many types of operations. They could survive in the wild and evade detection for ex-

tended periods. They could also hit hard and fast if
needed. A raid performed by the 101st Airborne's
LRRP platoon, that took place at the same time
Nam's Angels were motoring along the Cambodian
border, perhaps set the record for speed. The men,
led by Lieutenant Daniel McIsac, called it their
12-minute mission.

It started with Lieutenant McIsac tracing his
finger along a map for the benefit of his platoon,
stopping when he reached the Song Ve Valley.
Pointing to a small village he announced, "This is
our target." Intelligence claimed that a high-level
Viet Cong political officer used the village as a base
of operations. McIsac explained that the LRRPs
would land in the village, round up as many people
as possible, and hope that one of them was the
political officer. In the quest for information about

Captured —Troops with mine detectors inspect captured Viet Cong grain stocks—some of it stolen from the South Vietnamese— after a successful mission.

enemy activities, LRRPs often performed prisoner snatches. The target in such operations was usually an armed enemy soldier. The mission in the Song Ve Valley was more like a mass kidnapping, but orders were orders and so the LRRPs set out.

Minutes before dusk six helicopters roared into the village at tree-top level. As they set down, the 101st recon platoon realized they had caught the enemy by surprise. Black clad figures carrying weapons ran around in confusion. Most headed off into the near-by jungle. Best of all, shocked by the unexpected onslaught, none of the VC opened fire. They were too intent on running for their lives.

The paratroopers fanned out to begin searching the huts and farmyards for detainees. They concentrated on males of military age. Soon a few scattered shots rang out from the surrounding jungle. As the LRRPs continued the roundup, resistance increased. Clearly the VC were reorganizing. While the LRRPs were gathering the prisoners in the middle of the village, the fire grew in intensity. Fortunately the fading light made it difficult for the VC to fire accurately: "I could see the muzzle flashes in a draw (small ravine)" recalls an LRRP sergeant. Manning a machine gun, the sergeant returned fire. He knew he probably wouldn't hit anything, but he hoped to force the VC to keep their heads down while the helicopters returned to pick the patrol up.

The helicopters returned to hover just above the ground. It was a "hot" LZ and the pilots didn't want to hang around too long. The paratroopers pushed 15 villagers into the choppers and piled in themselves. They brought along a rucksack full of Chinese hand grenades, maps, and other documents found in the village. The helicopters climbed to safety. No American had been hit. The entire operation ended in 12 minutes.

The detainees were dropped off with the brigade's intelligence and interrogation team. The next day the pleased intelligence officers reported that among the detainees was the target of the raid, the Viet Cong's regional political indoctrination officer. Twelve minutes on the ground, no friendly losses, mission successful; the LRRPs could celebrate a near perfect mission.

Exploits like these often went unnoticed and unreported mainly because the LRRPs and rangers fought many small battles far away from friendly eyes. The rangers often wanted it this way. Never was this more the case than when an angry ranger went out on his one-man patrol.

The war had grown bitter. Both sides fought with increased ferocity. The ranger's unit had been taking losses. Feeling he had some scores to settle, the ranger went to his commanding officer and said: "I'm going out."

"When?" asked the officer.

"None of your business."

"How long?"

"None of your business," he repeated.

"Where should I look for you if you don't come back?" asked the officer.

Recalling the sight of tortured, mutilated comrades hung upside down in enemy-held villages, the ranger answered: "Don't worry about it. If I don't come back it's because there's nothing to find."

Five days later the ranger returned from his one-man patrol.

"Where did you go?" asked the commanding officer.

"None of your business."

"What's your body count?"

"None of your business."

The officer tried a different approach: "How many do you want credited to you?"

"It doesn't matter, three or three hundred."

Concerned, the officer asked: "Look, how do you feel?"

"All right," replied the ranger.

"Did you accomplish your mission?"

"Yes."

"That's good enough for me," concluded the officer.

Within a few months this ranger unit was pulled out of the field. The mutilation and atrocity incidents had gotten out of hand. The killing became savage. Many rangers, and American soldiers throughout Vietnam, kept score by cutting off the ears or fingertips of the fallen enemy, sewing the parts into necklaces, and defiantly wearing them. Here was a sign of the war's dark side. A doctor who cared for wounded American rangers and listened to their stories commented: "Nothing in the world is more frightening than an American soldier unchained from the bonds of discipline."

Captured —An instructor demonstrates a captured AK-47 to students at a ranger school. Slower and heavier than its US rival, the M-16, it proved more reliable in combat.

Tracker Force!

The Ho Chi Minh Trail

THE LONG RANGE reconnaissance patrol of the 173d Airborne had been on the ground for 24 hours. It was a humid August day in 1967. The five-man team proceeded cautiously through the mountainous terrain 20 kilometers northeast of Dak To Special Forces camp close to the Ho Chi Minh Trail, the principal enemy supply route. The assistant patrol leader, Sergeant Chester McDonald, served as point-man, constantly scanning the heavy brush ahead. Next came Sergeant Charles Holland, the patrol leader. He watched the right flank. The radioman followed and watched the left. The team scout walked behind him watching the right and scouting the right flank during stops. Specialist 4 Robert Brooks was responsible for rear security. He walked practically backwards, watching intently to see if anyone followed. If he saw something he would snap his fingers to alert the other four men and then communicate with them by hand signals. Brooks also covered the team's trail, smoothing out bent grass and erasing all signs of the patrol's passage. But it had rained the night before. The team's footprints in the soft ground could not be totally concealed. This worried Brooks.

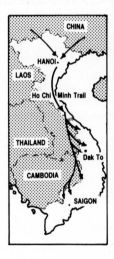

Sergeant Holland encouraged his men to remain vigilant. He expected contact at any time. Holland's mission was to head for a narrow, well-used trail that another LRRP had discovered two days previously and set up an observation post to watch for traffic on the trail. Only minutes before his team had boarded its helicopter, Holland had learned that six to eight Viet Cong had been observed from an aircraft within 1,000 meters of the proposed insertion point. When offered the chance to postpone the mission, Holland declined. Instead he chose a

slightly different landing zone. A day after landing, Holland's men had still not detected any recent signs of enemy activity. They had investigated two small bunker complexes and reckoned they were at least two weeks old. Eventually they set down their rucksacks in the middle of a small defensive perimeter on the designated hillside. In the center, the radioman set down his radio and raised the long antenna to communicate with base.

Ten minutes after arriving, Sergeant McDonald spotted three men walking along a small trail. Holland studied them through his binoculars and

Tracker Force!

TAIL GUNNER:
A rear scout of
Company H,
75th Rangers,
armed with an
M-16 rifle,
keeps watch
during a patrol
along the Dong
Nai River in
1970. Walking
or, sometimes,
crawling tail
was one of the
loneliest jobs
on a patrol.
With his back to
the rest of the
squad, out of
sight and often
out of
whispering
distance, a rear
scout could
easily become
separated from
his patrol as he
scoured the trail
for signs of
enemy
movement. In
the eerie silence
of a jungle, with
the constant
drone of hungry
mosquitoes, it
was a job that
called for a
calm, capable,
and self-
sufficient type
of soldier.

confirmed that the figures were enemy soldiers carrying rifles and rucksacks. As he watched, the group increased from 3 to 11, to 17, to 21. Holland ordered McDonald to contact the artillery on the radio and request a fire mission.

Specialist Brooks continued to watch the team's rear while the other four men concentrated on the enemy sighting. As the fire mission was being called, he heard a single rifle shot off in the distance. The sound of voices immediately followed. The voices were very, very close.

Brooks turned to give the warning signal for

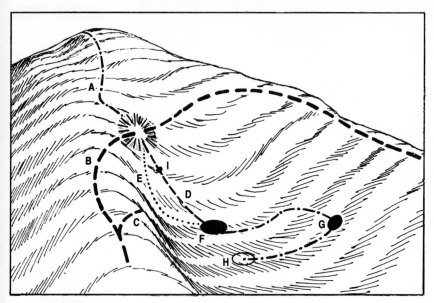

ANATOMY OF AN AMBUSH:

(A) The route taken by Holland's men. (B) The heavily used VC trail they spotted. (C) Small trail used by VC. (D) Withdrawal route used by Holland's team. (E) Brooks's withdrawal route. (F) Brooks rejoins team. (G) Team stops without Holland. (H) Exfiltration LZ. (I) Holland's body found here.

enemy to the rear. Devastating rifle fire and grenades exploded amidst the team's small perimeter. They were under attack from enemy soldiers hidden only 5 to 10 meters away. One of the first shots hit Brooks in the back. As he collapsed, Brooks may not have immediately realized what had happened. In spite of his efforts to conceal the patrol's trail, a VC tracker team had cleverly stalked the LRRPs. They had been skillful enough to move silently through the thick brush and get close to the LRRPs without being detected. The VC had then timed their attack perfectly, striking while most of the team was distracted by the target to the front. Brooks knew the team was in big trouble. He recovered quickly and fired back at the Viet Cong. He saw one black-pajama-clad figure stagger and topple over. Suddenly he realized he was alone with the enemy. The other four had gone.

The team had heard Brooks's warning just before the shooting started. One LRRP had turned toward the rear and engaged the hidden enemy. Sergeant Holland, who had been observing the enemy to the front when the attack came from the rear, immediately grabbed his assistant team leader and shoved him downslope while telling him to lead the patrol to safety. Holland then exchanged his binoculars for his rifle and opened fire to cover the retreat. The team scout sprinted past Holland. The sergeant yelled: "Keep going, I'll cover the rear!"

Hearing the shouts to run, the radioman tried to pick up his radio and take off. The long antenna hung up in the brush. Intense enemy fire stopped him from trying any further. The radioman left his radio and joined the others fleeing down the hill.

The LRRPs were now separated in three parts: Holland fighting a one-man rearguard, Brooks alone in his position, and McDonald leading the other two downslope away from the enemy. The three covered 200 meters before pausing in a clearing. Here Sergeant Holland rejoined them and ordered the radioman to call for help. The terrible news that the radio had been left behind had barely been comprehended when an English-speaking voice yelled out from the brush.

"Papa One, Papa One, I'm hit!" It was Brooks.

After Brooks had realized he was alone he staggered away from the intense enemy fire to the base of the hill. Spotting the others, he had yelled for help. Splashing through a marsh toward his comrades, Brooks fell, rose, and fell again. The radioman ran to him and helped Brooks rise to his feet. Heavy enemy fire continued to hit all around the LRRPs. But the VC were now acting in a very strange fashion. Huddled at the base of the hill, the team

SIGN HUNTER:
A ranger searches a trail for signs of recent enemy movement during a mission near Dalat. Although rangers received training in tracking skills, the Viet Cong were capable of fully exploiting the cover of the jungle. Even though Sgt. Holland's team scoured the jungle in all directions, the enemy managed to come within 15 feet before the fight began.

could hear them shouting "Number 10" and "De De." In addition, many of them were laughing and firing into the air. The LRRPs figured they must be high on some kind of narcotic.

Regardless of the apparent confused state of some of the Viet Cong, Holland recognized that there were enough enemy to wipe his men out. His team was without communications 20 kilometers from help. Two of his four men were wounded: Brooks with a serious back wound and a second fragmentation wound above his eye, and another soldier with a minor head wound from an enemy grenade. Huddled

Tracker Force!

SURVIVAL SKILLS:
The point man in an LRRP scans the jungle for signs of the enemy. Walking or often crawling, point was the most dangerous job on a patrol. Since it required constant vigilance the job was rotated frequently during the course of a patrol. The denser the jungle, and the more unmapped and hostile the terrain, the longer it took for a patrol to travel. A half a kilometer a day was not uncommon.

with his badly shocked team at the bottom of the hill, Holland tried to calm everyone, reassuring his men that they would be all right.

Then he ordered McDonald to lead them out while he covered the rear. The team scout heard his leader say something about "holding them off." He sensed that Holland was a bit off balance, flushed with the excitement of combat amidst the steady rain of enemy fire. The scout grabbed Holland by the arm and pleaded for the team to stay together. The sergeant jerked away and ran back up the hill. He had only his rifle with two 20-round magazines

Fully loaded —Weighed down by his pack, his M-16 at the ready, a ranger pauses by a tree during a three-day mission. The heaviest items in the 60-pound pack were rounds of ammunition and smoke and fragmentation grenades.

of ammunition and some grenades. At least 20 Viet Cong were firing from upslope.

As the team struggled along the side of an adjacent ridge, enemy fire continued to track them. Then the fire shifted away to the east. The Viet Cong were concentrating on the closest target—Sergeant Holland. Holland's efforts to draw enemy fire to cover his men's escape were working. As the team fled they heard the shooting dramatically intensify. It reached a crescendo in the area of the observation post. Then the firing stopped.

The team's commanding officer had been monitoring the radio during the entire operation. He had heard the LRRPs call for artillery. After that the radio went silent. As the commander took off in his helicopter he heard another LRRP team, operating some three kilometers from Holland's position, report hearing the sounds of small arms and grenades off in the distance. Thoroughly alarmed, the officer hastened to the scene. For 45 minutes he flew over the team's last known location. Finally, he spotted yellow smoke drifting up from the jungle. Hovering overhead he saw figures flashing a red panel. They were his men. The red panel meant they were still in contact with the enemy. The commander called for helicopter gunships.

The LRRPs had been hiding for 45 minutes. They were without communications 20 kilometers from the nearest friendly force. They tried to signal a nearby helicopter, not knowing it was their commander's, with a mirror and the colored signal panels. It didn't work. Growing desperate, Sergeant McDonald decided to release smoke grenades to attract the chopper's attention. Soon two helicopter gunships were delivering welcome suppressive fire all around the team. Following this preparation, a third chopper landed 50 meters away. The four made it to the rescue craft and lifted off.

That afternoon a reaction force from the Airborne Brigade returned to the battle scene. The four LRRPS went along to try to find Sergeant Holland. The next day they discovered his body 20 meters from the observation post. Like trained detectives on the scene of a homicide, the LRRPs reconstructed events from the clues strewn on the ground.

Evidently Holland had fought his way back to the post in an effort to recover the radio. He had carried

off as much equipment as possible and tried to destroy the remainder with grenades. On his body was some of the equipment he had recovered. It was very apparent that the sergeant had put up a tremendous last fight. The LRRPs found a fragment of his rifle near his body. It indicated that Holland had received a near-direct M-79 grenade hit. But he had sustained many nonfatal wounds before the lethal wound above his heart. The vegetation around his body was torn up and trampled, scuff and skid marks showed clearly in the damp soil. To the LRRPs who were trained to interpret such signs, it was obvious that Holland had engaged in hand-to-hand combat before falling.

The survivors also knew that their sergeant had sacrificed himself to save them. In the ensuing days, the four LRRPs carefully wrote out statements describing what had happened. In cooperation with their officers, they meticulously filled out the paper-work recommending that Sergeant Holland receive the Congressional Medal of Honor for his gallantry and self-sacrifice above and beyond the call of duty.

The request was turned down. A little less than eight months later, for his valor Sergeant Charles J. Holland was awarded a posthumous Distinguished Service Cross, the Army's second highest medal, during ceremonies at Fort Monmouth, New Jersey. In nearby Elizabeth, Holland's hometown, a playground was named in his honor.

Hell breaks loose

IT STARTED innocently enough. The National Police required some extra security in the Cholon suburb of Saigon. The city had witnessed intense combat during the surprise Tet Offensive at the end of January. With indications that the VC/NVA might try something again in late May 1968, the high command wanted to take extra precautions. So the 35th ARVN Ranger Battalion got the call, split its companies into combat teams, and established roadblocks throughout Cholon. For the men the assignment provided a welcome respite from jungle duty. The first night, guards at one of the checkpoints noticed two attractive teenage girls hanging about. Sensing an opportunity, they ordered the girls to come over and casually frisked them. To the rangers' surprise they found one carried a pistol while the other had several grenades taped to her body. The following day during a similar exercise at another roadblock, some rangers found two more teenage girls carrying weapons, including a sawn-off shotgun. Alerted to the fact that Saigon carried some of the same dangers as operations in the field, the rangers paid greater attention to their duty during the ensuing days. For 10 days nothing happened. On day 11 all hell broke loose.

Captain Robert Reitz, the battalion's senior advisor, was at the command post when the alert came over the radio: Take the unit to a heavily populated section of Cholon where a Vietnamese Marine unit was in a life-and-death struggle with an enemy force of unknown size. In consultation with the South Vietnamese commander, Reitz tried to piece together the extremely confused situation. Apparently a South Vietnamese Marine platoon was trapped on the top two floors of an apartment

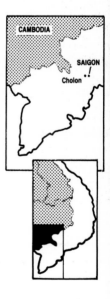

building. The VC controlled the lower floors as well as several adjacent buildings.

In cooperation with other units, an ARVN ranger company fought their way into the area to rescue the Marines. By the time they reached the apartment building only three Marines were left. It was a powerful foretaste of things to come.

A few days later on 1 June, the 35th Rangers received orders "to take the area in the least amount of time." Such orders were not designed to spare human flesh. Building by building the rangers drove into Cholon. The Viet Cong had turned each structure into a miniature fortress. They had knocked

Hell breaks loose

THE BATTLE FOR SAIGON:

A wounded ARVN ranger captain is hauled to safety as a combined American and South Vietnamese force comes under fire in the former French National Cemetery on the outskirts of Saigon. The ARVN rangers, considered to be the unit most loyal to the Saigon regime, had hoped that defending the capital would be less hazardous than life in the jungle. The tumult-filled days of mini-Tet proved otherwise.

holes in the walls of most of the buildings so that they could travel from building to building very quickly without being detected by the rangers confined to the streets below. In some homes the rangers found piles of face masks, a sign that the Viet Cong were swimming through the city's sewers. This explained how the Viet Cong were able to emerge behind ARVN lines and reoccupy buildings previously captured at a heavy price in ranger blood. The 35th's strength had already been whittled down by constant sniper fire combined with periodic short range firefights.

The rangers learned they were fighting the 6th

Captured —An ARVN ranger brandishes a captured Viet Cong B-40 rocket launcher captured during a sweep of the suburb of Cholon, Saigon's Chinese enclave. Armed with mortars and the shoulder-held B-40, the Viet Cong held out for several days until the rangers attacked with tanks.

Viet Cong Battalion, a unit supposedly destroyed in the Tet Offensive. Persevering, the 35th closed in on the VC from three sides. As the rangers burst into a room, the Viet Cong would hurl grenades and vanish using their specially prepared bolt holes. However, after five days of intense "dirty fighting," advisor Reitz believed that the rangers had taken the whole area. They physically occupied all but three buildings.

To clear these the South Vietnamese battalion commander summoned tank support. Psyching themselves up for the final assault, the rangers chanted "Kill VC, Kill VC" as they prepared to go in. To Reitz it was almost as if they were on drugs. With tanks leading the way, the "ranger-type assault" advanced against the last enemy stronghold.

The Viet Cong skillfully defended their position. The tanks halted at a safe point halfway to the three buildings. Now the rangers went to the front. They bypassed their own armor, and made a naked charge into a hail of fire. Two particularly deadly VC snipers practically stopped the assault by themselves. They fired in tandem and with each volley down went two rangers. Other Viet Cong fired B-40 rockets into the narrow streets. Each rocket knocked down another three or four rangers.

Seeing the 35th decimated, the advisor called the senior ranger commander: "We've got to get tanks out there or we will have a lot of dead rangers!"

"No can do," came the reply.

Frustrated at the lack of tank support, Reitz went to the South Vietnamese ranger colonel and pleaded with him to order the tanks in. Unable to direct the tanks via the radio, the colonel took matters into his own hands. Running up the bullet-splattered street where it seemed no one could survive, wearing a flak vest without a steel helmet, he reached the parked tank, climbed onto the deck, and pounded on the turret. A head emerged and the colonel began cursing the figure roundly. Galvanized into action, the tank rolled up the street once more. In its wake came another tank followed by the surviving rangers.

Suddenly a figure leaned out a window and dropped a satchel charge onto the back of a tank. The resultant explosion blew one crewman out of the vehicle, yet it kept going. The second tank took a rocket hit on its front armor plate. Shedding the blow, this tank also drove on. The tanks advanced three more blocks but it was useless. The ARVN rangers took fearful losses yet could not evict the Viet Cong defenders. Worse, hostile fire erupted behind the rangers from previously secured buildings. Somehow the Communists had infiltrated through ranger lines to threaten their rear. It took five more tanks to secure the street behind the 35th so the rangers could evacuate their wounded.

During the night ranger patrols captured three VC dressed in ARVN Marine uniforms who were trying to flee the area. Apparently enemy morale was low. Interrogation of the prisoners revealed that the VC battalion commander and executive officer were seriously wounded and the unit had suffered considerable losses. For the next two days the rangers pressed on. It continued to be "a nasty fight," with the remnants of the enemy force waiting until the rangers were at point-blank range. Only then did the Viet Cong use the last of their ammunition in a suicidal final defense.

Eventually the rangers conquered the bloody streets of Cholon. Believing that the local inhabitants had aided the enemy, the rangers took revenge, looting the houses. This breakdown in discipline did not overshadow the unit's gallant conduct during an extended period of terrible fighting. The battle showed the strengths and weaknesses of the South Vietnamese military under the merciless scrutiny of street fighting. On the down side there was lack of unit coordination, interservice rivalry exampled by the refusal of the tanks to support the rangers for fear of taking too many casualties that would look bad on an after-action report, and failure to completely secure an area before moving on. On the positive side there were episodes of outstanding courage including a one-man charge by the ranger colonel.

Many American LRRPs and rangers dismissed South Vietnamese fighting prowess, often with hatred. Too many times they felt let down at critical moments. As with any army, leadership in the South Vietnamese military was everything. Had American skeptics been present in the streets of Cholon during the bloody first days of May, they might have gained a new respect for the ARVN rangers.

Captured —A Viet Cong guerrilla captured during the fighting in mini-Tet. The brutal fighting nearly annihilated the VC units committed to Saigon.

Lessons learned

BY 1968, many ranger-type units throughout Vietnam had developed standard operating procedures based on hard experience. From the command perspective, a recurring issue was whether long-range reconnaissance patrols should be expected to engage in combat. Lieutenant Colonel Joseph Zummo, the commander of Company F, 51st Infantry, described his unit's purpose as primarily strategic reconnaissance and only secondarily target acquisition. His LRRPs were not intended for combat. However, if "compromised"—the colonel's term for the often desperate situations that arose when the enemy discovered his men's position—Company F had orders to engage regardless of the size of the enemy force.

Ideally Company F would silently patrol the countryside, gliding from concealed position to concealed position while they observed enemy troop movements and located hostile base camps. The information the patrols collected would be analyzed by intelligence officers who tried to anticipate the enemy's intentions. Depending on the situation, artillery, air strikes, and B-52 bomber raids would be directed against the targets the LRRPs had found. In reality, both the higher command and the men on the ground were often tempted to overlook the recon role and instead engage the enemy.

On one occasion a six-man patrol led by a sergeant noted for his aggressive attitude was on a trail-watch mission. They discovered a complete VC/NVA battalion. After counting 322 enemy soldiers, and still not seeing the end of the enemy column, the sergeant "got tired of waiting," blew his claymore mines sited along the trail, and ran. Knowing that regular units spent endless hours beating the bush

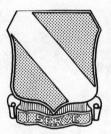

Insignia of Troop F, 51st Infantry

99

and failing to find the enemy, the LRRPs—who frequently made enemy contact—often had trouble merely observing an enemy target and letting it pass without drawing blood.

It was against this background that Zummo tried to systematize the engagement procedure. When his patrols found a target, they were to radio a description of the situation to the colonel. He would then authorize them to engage or avoid contact. Typically a message came that a patrol saw four enemy

Lessons learned

IN-COUNTRY PROCEDURE:

Toting 60-pound field packs, an LRRP patrol from F Company, 75th Rangers, moves Indian-file across a small river during a three-day search-and-destroy mission. Before moving out, each ranger taped down the most frequently gripped parts of his weapon, here a Colt Commando sub-machine gun (inset) to reduce the risk of making any sound that might give away his position to the enemy. This shortened version of the M-16 had a longer flash suppressor to make it harder for the enemy to pinpoint a ranger's position.

soldiers coming along a trail. Zummo would tell them to engage, but would warn them they would not be extracted after the fight. While tough on his men, this procedure ensured that a patrol would not deliberately bring on a fight in order to be pulled out of the field.

Similarly, Zummo did not let the plea "we're out of ammo" serve as an excuse to extract a unit. If a unit got low on ammo he arranged a helicopter re-supply mission. His patrols had a five-day mission

Lessons learned

SPOT CHECK: A member of F Company, 75th Rangers, checks map coordinates during a three-day mission. Map reading in the horizonless world of triple-canopy jungle was almost impossible; with nothing but a dense canopy of interwoven branches overhead, patrols often went for days without seeing any distinctive landmarks. Frequently LRRPs could not pinpoint their positions to less than half a kilometer.

to stay in the field. The only time Zummo altered the mission length was when a unit became dangerously "compromised." Even then, after the patrol was extracted by helicopter they would be re-inserted somewhere nearby that same day. Zummo felt that the fact a patrol had become engaged meant that there were good targets in that area. Therefore, the patrol should continue. Furthermore, the five-day clock was reset when the unit was reinserted! This meant that if a unit had been out three days, became engaged, and needed rescuing, it would be put back in as soon as possible for a further five days. The LRRPs in Company F, 51st Infantry, were not permitted to leave the field until they finished their mission.

Listen good —Members of the Company F, 51st Infantry, long-range patrol receive a briefing on a surveillance and ambush operation during January 1968. During that year officers tightened up on discipline to transform the 51st's LRRPs into crack outfits.

The company generally tried to keep 12 patrols out at a time. Ninety percent of these were "light patrols" consisting of five or six men. Anything bigger was termed a "heavy patrol." The 10 percent that went out on these heavy patrols had a different type of mission. They were sent into areas of heavy enemy contact and ordered "to mix it up," inflict as much damage as possible, try to snatch a prisoner, strip the killed of any documents, and move away. To provide the firepower to conduct such operations, the heavy patrols each carried an M-60 machine gun.

Typically when sending out a light patrol, Zummo received orders to monitor a certain trail junction. He passed this order on to the team. Recognizing that the LRRPs needed to operate independently, the colonel left it up to the team to plan the details. He only insisted that they carry a radio and enough water and food for five days.

Two choppers, called "slicks," handled the insertion of a light patrol. One carried the men, while the other remained empty to cover emergencies. A helicopter gunship flew escort duty to protect the slicks during the dangerous landing operation. If a helicopter was shot down during a mission, the patrol was supposed to secure the crash site. The empty reserve chopper would land to rescue the pilot and equipment from the downed bird. Only when another helicopter arrived would the LRRPs be extracted. A hard priority—pilot, equipment, men—justified by Zummo on the grounds that his men were trained to survive in the jungle and the whole

Lessons learned

JUNGLE BREAK: Their eyes darkened with camouflage rings, members of an LRRP team from the 75th Rangers take a break during a patrol. Although issued with the standard three-pound helmet, most rangers preferred bush hats that softened a man's features so that he blended in with the jungle, or went bareheaded except for sweatbands cut from green parachute silk. The RTO (center) has his radio aerial bent down to prevent it snagging on a branch.

rescue should only take 15 to 30 minutes anyway. If the landing went without trouble, the chopper would be on the ground, or hover just above it, for only three to five seconds. In another five seconds the LRRPs disappeared into cover and their five-day mission began.

Within 10 kilometers of the insertion point was a radio relay post, usually unmanned. In addition an aerial relay station flew overhead. When the patrol was in position, it sent a message through

these relays so its location could be accurately pinpointed. Since the men invariably operated within
range of friendly artillery, the radio link gave them
access to instant firepower. Frequently, while on the
move, the LRRPs were unable to pinpoint their
positions within half a kilometer. Such uncertainty
made coordination with nearby friendly units difficult. Too often the LRRPs found themselves arriving in position overlooking a trail only to hear a
friendly armored column approach. Roaring along,

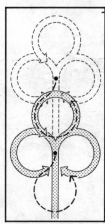

Search pattern —The cloverleaf search involved one man staying at a central point while the rest of the squad fanned out around him making circular searches in four directions. If no one encountered anything untoward, the patrol would move forward and the pattern would be repeated.

"reconning by fire"—shooting blindly into the underbrush to disrupt a potential enemy ambush—the armor had no idea that Americans were out there. Even if a trooper on an M-113 armored personnel carrier saw an LRRP, he probably would think the well-camouflaged figure was a Viet Cong. Friendly fire was one of many hazards endured by the LRRPs.

When moving through the jungle, a patrol often performed "cloverleaf" searches. One soldier stayed at a central point while the others looped out in search patterns covering all four directions. Moving in this fashion, a patrol might cover only half a kilometer a day. But it was a thorough, safer approach than merely marching along in column. After moving as silently as possible to a new position, the patrol sat down to watch and wait.

They hid so well that enemy soldiers could pass within 10 meters of their position and not see them. The flip side of this was that once they were seen—compromised—the resultant fight began at incredibly close range. If they could make it to a landing zone, they could be pulled out quickly by helicopters kept on call for just this purpose. Although no one liked to perform night extractions, the half light available in the early morning or late evening hours were preferred by most. Each patrol carried a strobe light and flares to reveal their position to the rescue choppers. Consequently, night extractions were no real problem.

All of this became standard operating procedure (SOP) for the men in Company F. Other LRRPs and rangers had similar SOPs. Things could go wrong. The trail junction clearly seen on a map might be impossible to find on the ground because it had become so overgrown. The life-preserving radio might not work at a critical time. The rescue helicopter might not be able to find the landing zone because of rain or fog. Or maybe the company had been operating in the same area too long. "Charlie," as the VC were nicknamed, could adjust to LRRP tactics. He was a veteran soldier too. Sometimes when the 51st stayed in an area for more than 30 days they would pick up report papers from the enemy dead addressed to higher headquarters. These reports accurately detailed the LRRP's SOP. When this happened, Zummo observed, "I knew Charlie had me down pat and it was time to get out

Lessons learned

JUNGLE FATIGUE: His face showing signs of exhaustion, M-16 ammunition clips slung diagonally in canvas pouches across his chest, a smoke grenade canister and two one-pound ''baseball'' grenades clipped to his waist, a member of C Company, 75th Rangers, returns to base after a mission. Frequently the hard-worked LRRP teams had less than 24 hours rest before going back on patrol.

Lessons learned

UNDER FIRE:
Forced to dive for cover into the soft yellow mud of a riverbank, men of N Company, 75th Rangers, wait while their radioman reports their position after coming under enemy mortar fire near Xuan Loc in 1970.

of there." The Viet Cong and North Vietnamese placed an equally high value on accurate intelligence, frequently gathered by reconnaissance patrols. A North Vietnamese veteran who "rallied" to the Allied cause described how his unit conducted such operations:

> We start the day at 0430 or 0530. . . . The special equipment we usually carry consists of radios, maps, compasses, binoculars, notebook, and a knife. I inspect every man . . . his weapon, ammunition (90 rounds per man), two grenades, and equipment prior to departure. We move out at 0600. During movement to the reconnaissance objective, we usually travel about three kilometers per hour, taking a 10

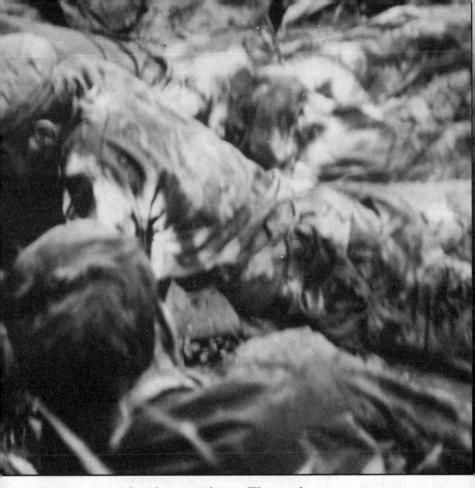

to 15 minute break every hour. We rarely travel more than a day and a half without sleeping.

At 1500 hours we find a place to make camp for the night. When we arrive at the reconnaissance objective, we usually establish a post approximately one or two hours' distance from the objective. Next we dispatch small teams (two or three men) to move in as close to the objective as possible. If we possibly can, we try to penetrate and enter the objective area to determine the exact enemy strength and location. We try to locate and count the number of heavy weapons. . . . If we are successful and are not detected we withdraw using the same route.

Traveling light
—A Viet Cong
guerrilla
carrying an
AK-47 and
wearing a
camouflage
cloak made
from salvaged
US parachute
material patrols
along a
ridgeline.
Compared to
the heavily
armed rangers,
the VC traveled
light.

We are never assigned a straight combat mission to engage the enemy. We are only told to observe and report what we have seen. . . . One of my reconnaissance squads saw a a US reconnaissance team on three different occasions. Each time I ordered my men to hold their fire and not to engage US troops unless we were discovered. US reconnaissance teams always fire into suspected positions and this is not effective . . . when they fire all we have to do is bypass them. Often we are able to determine the reconnaissance objective of the US team because of these mistakes.

Communist patrols traveled light. During a mission they had little time for sleep. Faced with the decision whether to engage or not, the VC/NVA scout patrols chose to avoid contact in order to pursue their primary mission of reconnaissance. This was the same as the standard procedure for the American LRRPs. A striking difference in the way the opposing sides operated was that the VC/NVA patrols went to assigned locations knowing the Allies would be there. It was the Allies who manned fixed fortifications protecting camps, depots, and bases year after year. Even when the Allies entered the field on one of their large operations, their presence was soon detected by the VC/NVA. The American LRRPs/rangers set off not knowing where the enemy was. Usually they undertook an operation with limited information or intelligence reports they had little faith in. They had to both find the enemy and avoid detection. All their counterparts on the other side had to do was avoid detection.

It was not always easy. Sergeant Mike Daniels, leader of the 196th Light Infantry Brigade's LRRP, had planned to avoid enemy detection during one three-day patrol. However, shortly after his men landed and completed a short hike to an observation post on a hillside, they heard shots from across the ridge. Daniels recognized the sounds as American weapons. He realized that another LRRP team was on the far side of the hill. There was a possibility that their shots were meant as a signal to Daniels's team. The sergeant ordered his men to fire a few shots into the air in acknowledgment. This prompted a heavy outbreak of gunshots mixed with the sound of exploding grenades. Several anxious minutes passed as Daniels pondered what to do. Suddenly a hard-pressed LRRP team emerged on the crest of the hill and a helicopter appeared to extract them. Daniels's team was alone. He began to wonder if his firing had given away his position.

Soon his worst fears were confirmed. Sniper rounds started to smack into the ground around his men. The team called for artillery fire. The shelling silenced the sniper fire. Knowing they were in for a long night, the men of the 196th LRRP team set out trip flares and claymores all around their position. The sun set and it became dark. Eventually they saw two flashlights bobbing around the area where their helicopter had landed that afternoon. It was an enemy tracker team. "We just watched and held our breath," recalls Daniels, "we didn't want to make contact and could only hope they wouldn't see us in the dark."

His hope proved vain. A moving figure approached the LRRP position. One of the LRRPs fired an illumination flare. The flarelight revealed two Viet Cong. The patrol fired, killing them instantly. This brought on a fusillade of fire from other VC who had remained at the bottom of the slope while their two scouts probed for the Americans. Daniels called for help. Two helicopter gunships charged into the fight, machine guns blazing. Enemy fire struck one of the choppers, knocking one of its machine guns from its mount. As a result, machine gun bullets sprayed wildly all over the slope. The LRRPs hugged the ground as American bullets swept through their position. Having experienced nothing but bad luck since they had landed, the patrol finally caught a break. No one was hit and the fire seemed to discourage the VC, who retreated into the forest.

Daniels called for artillery fire to pursue the enemy. Under cover of its fire, the patrol jogged along the slope to another position. They settled down to wait, with the hope of all long range reconnaissance patrols: "Don't let us be found."

Although the team heard whispered talk all around them that night, the enemy could not pinpoint the American position. The next morning the Viet Cong were gone. After a terrifying start, the remainder of the three-day mission proceeded uneventfully.

Insignia of the 196th Light Infantry —In one classic incident two of its LRRP teams stumbled across each other in the jungle, tried signaling their relative positions by gunfire, and only succeeded in alerting the enemy to their positions.

From LRRP to ranger

Supporting the patrols

THE SMALL OBSERVATION airplane had been airborne for only a few minutes on an August evening in 1969 when the emergency message came. A 1st Division LRRP was in trouble. Lieutenant Woody Arnold's Eagle Watch flight immediately diverted toward the scene. Arnold, an aerial artillery observer with the 1st Division, had the mission to direct artillery fire from his perch in a 0-1 Birddog light aircraft. A 10-minute flight brought the Birddog over the troubled patrol's last known position.

Darkness had fallen. The patrol radioed that they had been discovered and an overwhelming enemy force was hot on their tail. They were running but they weren't sure they were going to make it. Arnold asked them to place a strobe light, used for nighttime signalling, in the barrel of one of their grenade launchers and point it toward the plane. This would allow him to pinpoint the patrol's position without broadcasting the light to the enemy watching on the ground. Flying at 1,500 feet the pilot switched his position lights on for a brief moment to give the LRRPs an aiming point. The strobe came on. Woody Arnold peered down through the darkness, straining to pick out familiar landmarks. He recognized the terrain and consulted his map. Quickly he radioed target coordinates to nearby artillery batteries.

Arnold directed the rounds so that they created an exploding protective steel curtain between the LRRPs and their pursuers. He kept in constant touch with the patrol. The enemy was so close that the LRRP radioman talked in a whisper or merely responded to Arnold's questions by clicking the microphone and breaking squelch: one click meaning yes, two meaning no. Together they adjusted the

Insignia of the 1st Division

From LRRP to ranger

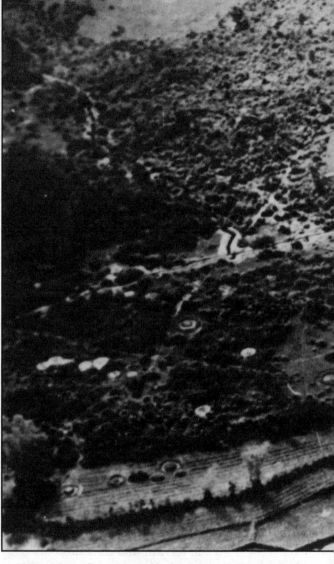

TARGET SPOTTER:
A forward air controller (FAC) flies an 0-1 Birddog spotter plane during a search-and-destroy mission. Flying an 0-1, FAC Woody Arnold was able to locate an LRRP team in danger of being overrun, summon firepower support, and direct a helicopter to rescue the patrol. Cruising at low altitudes looking for the enemy, FACs, who could operate on the same FM waveband as LRRPs, were often the only link between a stranded patrol and its base. The job was dangerous. More FACs were killed in Vietnam than any other type of pilot.

artillery fire. Soon more help arrived on station. Arnold directed helicopter gunships and "Puff the Magic Dragon," an Air Force C-47 equipped with rapid-fire miniguns and flares, to the aid of the beleaguered men on the ground. Despite the barrage from above, the Viet Cong continued to press in against the LRRPs. Firing their rifles, the LRRPs barely managed to keep the enemy at bay. Any moment the next enemy onslaught could overrun them. Since the patrol was hopelessly compromised, with

the Viet Cong knowing exactly where they were, the
decision was made to airlift the patrol out of the
area.

Arnold picked a large nearby clear area for the
rescue. He had the artillery bombard the clearing
to drive off any VC and to detonate any mines or
booby traps. Since the LRRPS had great difficulty
seeing their way through the dense foliage, other
batteries fired flares to illuminate the way to the
clearing. The gunships and artillery also peppered

115

Specialist or special skills? —A ranger undergoing rappel training at An Khe. Some officers believed that the Army's needs would be better served by training infantrymen in special skills rather than having a separate group of specialists.

the enemy position to prevent pursuit. The whole operation was orchestrated flawlessly by the aerial observer. By flarelight the patrol reached the clearing just as the helicopter arrived. Nobody panicked, everyone remained cool-headed, and in storybook-like tradition, the helicopter rescued the patrol in the nick of time. For his skillful conduct, Woody Arnold received the Air Medal with "V" for valor. More importantly, he had the immense satisfaction of knowing his actions had helped save the patrol.

Long-range reconnaissance patrols relied upon skill and cunning to avoid enemy detection. Once compromised they would run as long as they could. When all else failed and they could run no more, they turned to the tenuous link their radio gave them with the outside world. Then it was up to the helicopter, gunship, ground attack, and observation pilots and crew, as well as the artillerymen and aerial observers, to work in seamless cooperation so that the patrol on the run could survive.

Not everyone was sold on the LRRP concept. In the summer of 1968, one experienced lieutenant colonel with the elite 173d Airborne Brigade used his departure from Vietnam to criticize Army use of LRRPs. In an outspoken interview, he called for the abolition of LRRPs. While recognizing the value of long-range patrols as an early-warning buffer to prevent enemy surprise attacks, he felt that patrols should be platoon and company size, rather than five- and six-man LRRP teams, and that they could be formed using regular infantrymen rather than specialists.

As a military tool, the LRRPs had to be assessed by comparing gains they made against the resources consumed to accomplish that gain. The colonel reckoned that over a six-month period the brigade's LRRPs had generated only two really worthwhile contacts. Yet during the entire period helicopter transport and gunship resources were constantly on call supporting the LRRPs. He didn't "believe that the LRRPs over here are worth what we put into them."

Much of the problem was a matter of experience and leadership. The brigade's LRRPs didn't have anyone "who can take them in...and teach them to stay, when they are 30 meters from something that's going on." Without experienced leaders who knew

when to sit tight, even when the enemy came very close, and when to fire and run, the colonel found himself ordering helicopters in "to extract them because they hear bushes snapping; I extract them because they hear voices talking, I extract them for all sorts of things." The colonel believed the LRRP concept was a waste of assets and should be abolished.

He placed some of the blame on himself and others in brigade headquarters. There was so much pressure from higher up the chain of command to have all units active in the field that the brigade had no reserves available. Lacking a reaction force the brigade couldn't respond to an LRRP contact by sending in powerful ground reinforcements to smash the enemy. Consequently, even when the LRRPs did good work nothing came of it.

Many officers disagreed with the colonel's criticisms, but the criticisms underscored an essential requirement for a long-range reconnaissance

From LRRP to ranger

PUFF THE MAGIC DRAGON

Crew members of an AC-47 Dragonship fire their miniguns at targets on the ground 4,000 feet below in support of a ranger patrol under fire. Known first as Puff the Magic Dragon and later given the call sign Spooky, the fixed-wing Dragonship had three miniguns located on its left side. Operated electrically, each gun could spit out 7.62mm bullets at the rate of 300 per second—6,000 per minute.

patrol's success. A patrol needed veteran, experienced leaders. A leader had to be able to silently move the patrol through testing terrain day after day. His men in turn had to trust him to the point that they would remain motionless while overwhelming numbers of enemy soldiers marched by almost within touching distance. Until a man participated in enough patrols to be able to know instinctively when to fire, when to remain still, and when to run, he had to rely on his patrol leader. This

was a heavy demand upon both the leaders and the led. Regardless of a man's bravery, potential leadership abilities, and training, there was no substitute for a well-honed "jungle" sense. Without this sense, a patrol could be annihilated in a heartbeat.

ONE OF THE important ways the American military maintains its fighting traditions is through a system of lineage and honors. A unit traces its history, or lineage, back through time to an original

The insignia of Merrill's Marauders, a famous World War II era unit that was incorporated into the 75th Rangers.

parent unit. For example, 23 infantry regiments' lineages extend back to the Civil War. Battle honors can also be tracked back through the course of time. A modern soldier may learn that his predecessors have distinguished themselves at the Battle of the Bulge, the Argonne Forest, and Gettysburg. By keeping traditions alive the Army hopes to inspire its soldiers to emulate gallant, historical deeds.

In Vietnam the traditions passed on through the lineage and honor system were reinforced by the use of unit shoulder patches, flags with battle streamers, and regimental distinctive insignias. The colorful insignias sometimes included stirring mottos. The LRRP units attached to the 4th Infantry and 101st Airborne Divisions were known as "The Patriots" with the motto "Love of Country." The 9th and 25th Infantry Division's LRRP insignias showed a dolphin over the words "Play the Game" while the units working with the American Division and 199th Infantry Brigade had the simple motto "I Serve."

Since there were no separate ranger units, the proud ranger tradition was continued via the Special Forces, the so-called Green Berets. The Green Berets were given the right to claim the battle honors earned by rangers in earlier wars. The recon units on the other hand had no common designation or historical connection. As time passed the Army decided to change this and group the recon units together instead of having them fragmented among different infantry divisions. Since they all performed similar functions, a parent unit was needed to give the LRRPs a shared identity. In January 1969, the 75th Infantry became the LRRPs' parent unit with 13 ranger companies serving in Vietnam designated C-I and K-P. While their personnel stayed the same and the duties did not change, henceforth the recon units would be known as rangers.

When the Army cast about to find an appropriate parent ranger unit, it wanted to perpetuate old lineages and their traditions rather than create new ones. The 75th Infantry's past included Merrill's Marauders, a World War II era unit that had served in Burma, carrying out long-range penetration missions deep into the jungle. The 75th was a natural choice for the American rangers in Vietnam.

The Army was happy with this consolidated,

streamlined organization. The ranger companies now shared the same history, lineage, honors, and insignia. However, they continued to operate under the command and control of the various higher head-quarters to which they were attached. In practice the change made little difference to the small teams out in the field. Whether they were called rangers or LRRPs, they were tough.

SOUNDING OFF:
Sgt. Rick Hanbury of N Company, 75th Rangers, welcomes the dawn with his native bagpipes.

The cowboys

Training the ARVN

THE CROWD of South Vietnamese rangers hoisted the two American advisors onto their shoulders. Although the language was foreign, Sergeant Tom S. Cueto thought he understood the message conveyed by the many enthusiastic voices. The excited, happy rangers were expressing heartfelt affection for their newly arrived comrades and leaders. Glancing over at his fellow advisor, a stalwart Texan named Jeff Jager, Cueto couldn't help grinning. What a way to go to war, carried by the natives for presentation to the tribal chief, Major Tran, the commander of the 61st Ranger Company. Reaching the major's hootch, the rangers lowered Cueto and Jager to the ground. Collecting themselves, the advisors got a fast introduction to the fact that everything was not quite as it seemed. During the triumphant march from helicopter to command post the rangers had neatly stolen their advisors' watches and wallets. It was only the first in a series of rude surprises in store for the young advisors.

The fact that the two found themselves assigned to the ARVN rangers was unusual in itself. They had arrived in-country in 1969 at a time when American troops were already being pulled out of the war. The US Army seemed unable to decide what to do with them. Cueto was college-educated, trained for combat, qualified as an expert marksman, and had attended the Army's intelligence school. Except for the college education, Jager matched his credentials. With the dilution of the American Army by increasingly unwilling draftees, such soldiers were in short supply in Vietnam. Yet for the past few weeks they had bumped around from airport to replacement center to headquarters, performing such useful tasks as sweeping floors and

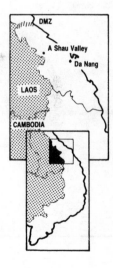

scrubbing latrines at the 90th Replacement Battalion.

Finally someone in the 23d American Division recognized the men's potential. An officer called them in to announce: "I have good news and I have bad news. First thing is you are both promoted to sergeant. The bad news is you're assigned to the intelligence detachment at Da Nang." Arriving in Da Nang they cooled their heels for a solid day and a half waiting for someone from the detachment to

The cowboys

VILLAGE PATROL:
A patrol of ARVN rangers armed with M1 carbines and vertical-feed Thompson .45 submachine guns move through a village in search of the Viet Cong in early 1962. At this stage ARVN forces had to make do with World War II vintage weapons. It was only when US forces were gradually withdrawn in the late 1960s that ARVN rangers received more up-to-date weaponry.

pick them up. Then they learned that due to the shortage of combat-qualified officers, selected sergeants were being assigned as advisors to South Vietnamese units. The promised "bad news" had happened. And that was how the two young, green Americans found themselves facing the suave, experienced Major Tran of the South Vietnamese rangers.

In late 1969 in northernmost I Corps, American advisors did not wear any indication of rank. This

125

Overkill —Forward observers check their position as a column of ARVN rangers moves into the jungle near Dong Xuci. During the course of the war, some ARVN ranger units developed into fine combat units.

kept South Vietnamese officers from losing face when receiving advice from their advisors who were considerably lower ranking. The system meant that two jumped-up sergeants new to Vietnam and new to combat could deal on even terms with a veteran ranger major such as Tran. In theory the Americans advised the rangers about important tactical considerations such as nighttime defense perimeters and helicopter assaults. But the advisors quickly learned that such subjects meant very little to a unit that seldom ventured out into the field.

Instead of operating like the American rangers, in small recon units inserted into hostile country, the ARVN rangers acted in company-sized and battalion formations. The enemy could usually evade such clumsy, large formations. Furthermore, the 61st Ranger Company spent most of its time in base. Cueto marvelled at how the rangers strutted around camp in freshly starched, tailor-made tiger fatigues and showed little concern about the war going on around them. He felt disgust at how their leader bartered away their rations and weapons on the black market, at how the men offered their wives to the advisors in return for small favors. He did recognize that the rangers had many combat skills. They handled their weapons well. Major Tran seemed to understand war and appeared to have the potential to be an excellent officer. Yet the advisor concluded that they were more a political force than an elite combat unit.

Being new to the war, Sergeant Cueto couldn't know that what he was observing were signs of combat fatigue, a poorly motivated group of men tired of endless war without results. All ARVN units went through a series of American advisors as the years passed. From the South Vietnamese perspective, the advisors came and went, and whether anyone listened to them was a matter of great indifference. They had been fighting before the Americans came and they would apparently have to continue the fight now that the Americans were pulling out. The individual ranger could see little reason to risk his life when it really didn't seem to matter. The ARVN rangers knew that their American counterparts, the US rangers, hated them.

The 61st Ranger Company saw no reason to pay attention to their newest advisors except when they needed them to call for helicopters. During one of the infrequent field operations, the first the new advisors participated in, a few men from the company were injured. Major Tran asked the advisors to call for a medevac flight, known by its call sign as a "dust-off." The Americans could play God, choosing when to call for a dust-off and who would be evacuated. Tran begged the advisors to call for the medevac choppers, claiming "many bad wounds, many bad wounds." Sergeant Cueto complied, the helicopters came, and one was shot down. As the advisors helped the wounded rangers to the surviving helicopter, they realized the men had only superficial wounds: scratches and cuts but nothing serious. Not surprisingly the relationship between the advisors and the rangers was "piss poor" in view of such occurrences.

Although the American military had been unable to instill a desire for combat in the 61st Company, certain American values had bridged the cultural gap. It seemed to be the heartfelt desire of every ranger in the company to be a cowboy from Texas. Consequently they took a real shining to the genuine article, Sergeant Jager. The Texan was an expert in judo and karate. He started giving a fighting class designed to teach the rangers how to be cowboys. One day before class he approached Cueto: "Tom, one of those bastards stole my wallet again."

"Well, don't worry about it," Cueto replied. Cueto forgot all about his fellow advisor's anger as he and Major Tran boarded a helicopter to go to Da Nang. The trip took longer than expected and the two didn't return until late in the evening. A senior ranger sergeant greeted them at the camp gate. The camp was empty and the sergeant was very excited. He explained what had happened.

As near as Cueto and Tran could make out, advisor Jager—still fuming over the thieving, ungrateful rangers—had taken a few drinks to calm down. Then inspiration struck and he decided to give the men a class in night combat patrolling. Jager ordered the rangers to fall in. Standing in line, the rangers listened as the Texan began his lecture. The senior Vietnamese sergeant translated: "Men, I'm going to teach you how to be John Waynes, real cowboys from Texas."

The rangers shifted their weight uneasily. But as

Insignia of the ARVN rangers —Despite wearing the symbol of a snarling panther, ARVN rangers did not always display the attitude of a ferocious fighting force. One advisor recalled being asked to call in a medevac helicopter for men with only superficial wounds.

The cowboys

MAIL CALL: The commanding officer of a Vietnamese ranger company distributes maps and mail to members of his unit before they begin a drive against the Viet Cong. Experience showed that the further a man fought from his village, the worse he fought. Wholesale desertions were not uncommon; the Vietnamese found it hard to understand the notion of collective security and often could only be relied upon to fight well when defending the land they were raised on.

they realized the Texan had their best interests at heart they relaxed.

"Now real cowboys have to be able to drink," Jager explained. The advisor demonstrated what he meant and soon the alcohol flowed freely throughout the company. Primed for action, Jager continued his instruction.

"You can't be cowboys unless you look like cowboys." The rangers nodded eagerly. "You're going to have to take off those uniforms." The unit

complied and stripped naked. "But of course cowboys wear six-shooters, so empty your holsters and put them on." Standing more or less in straight ranks, the rangers slung their empty pistol holsters. Jager taught them a simple, profane marching song in English, a chant to repeat in quick cadence.

"Okay. You can drink like cowboys, you look like cowboys, and you can sing like cowboys. We're moving out!"

The eager rangers followed Jager out of camp. The

People detector —A signalman sets up an antipersonnel short-range sensor on the perimeter of a hilltop fire support base. But despite being provided with an array of sophisticated electronic devices for detecting the enemy, US commanders realized that these devices could never be an effective substitute for men on the ground.

mission: a practice night assault against a nearby American camp. The camp housed a large American Military Police force.

Singing their newly learned chant, naked except for their holsters, the rangers assaulted the MPs' camp. Fistfights broke out everywhere. Eventually the burly American MPs subdued the rangers, locking the whole group up. It was this situation that Cueto and Major Tran encountered upon returning to base. An extremely irate American MP captain shouted at them that he had approximately 120 raving lunatics belonging to the 61st Rangers behind barbed wire, trussed up like prisoners, with the overflow secured in empty shipping containers.

Talking fast, Cueto negotiated to get the cowboy rangers and their intrepid advisor released. To finalize the deal and to ensure the incident would be hushed up, he had to give the MP captain some VC flags and NVA belt buckles. With throbbing heads and not a few bruises from their combat with the police, the deflated cowboys returned to base.

Shortly after the 61st South Vietnamese Ranger Company received its instructions on how to be a cowboy, two missions conducted by the 75th Rangers demonstrated the delicate balance between success and failure in the field.

One involved five soldiers belonging to Ranger Team 45, Company H, 75th Rangers, which was part of the 1st Cav's long-range reconnaissance force. In the beginning of November 1969, remote sensors surrounding one of the division's fire support bases detected a substantial increase in enemy activity. While machines could sense movement using seismic and infrared readings as well as chemical "sniffing," it took men on the ground to determine what was really going on. A warning order to prepare for a mission to monitor trail activity in the thick jungle outside Fire Support Base (FSB) Buttons went to the team led by Sergeant Milford Harvey.

The team spent the morning checking their gear. The equipment common to all included 8 quarts of water, 5 LRRP ration meals, grenades for the M-79 grenade launcher as well as 11 personal grenades, 2 claymore mines, 6 flares, and a map, air recognition panel, mirror, flashlight, compass, and wristwatch. In addition to their personal weapons,

The cowboys

RETRIEVED:
A senior US advisor examines a 129A Remington hand pump shotgun recaptured from the Viet Cong by an ARVN ranger during operations at An Xuyen in 1967. Although the Viet Cong received Soviet-manufactured small arms from the North, they relied heavily on capturing ARVN and US weapons to restock their armory. Captured weapons were often copied in VC underground factories.

The cowboys

SETTING UP AN AMBUSH:

After sensors reported an enemy buildup, a five-man patrol, Ranger Team 45, were given the task of ambushing the NVA and taking a prisoner for interrogation. After overflying the area and locating two parallel tracks, the team landed and made their way to the ambush point where they set up claymores to create a kill zone.

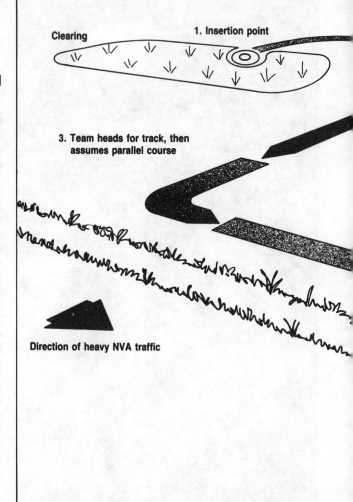

Clearing

1. Insertion point

3. Team heads for track, then assumes parallel course

Direction of heavy NVA traffic

the radioman and medic carried equipment vital to performing their special tasks.

In the early afternoon Ranger Team 45 made a brief overflight of the area to locate a landing zone. They made final preparations. The plan called for the team to land near a jungle treeline and rush into the nearby underbrush. They would wait 10 minutes for a security and communication check, watching the clearing to determine if the enemy had seen them arrive and establishing radio contact with

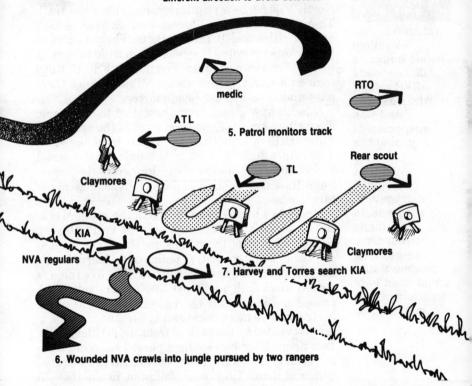

2. Security halt and communications check

4. Team swings wide of track to approach from different direction to avoid detection

medic

RTO

ATL

5. Patrol monitors track

Rear scout

TL

Claymores

KIA

Claymores

NVA regulars

7. Harvey and Torres search KIA

6. Wounded NVA crawls into jungle pursued by two rangers

supporting forces. If discovered, the team would be extracted immediately.

At 1600 hours the team made the short flight to the landing zone. As the lift helicopter made final descent, the assistant team leader spotted down below a hard-packed, heavily traveled trail about one meter wide running near the clearing. The rangers landed, made the required security and communications checks, and headed for the trail.

After finding the trail, Sergeant Harvey led them

Taken prisoner —With his hands bound, a disconsolate ARVN ranger who deserted and was suspected of joining the enemy undergoes initial interrogation. US advisors constantly stressed the need to take prisoners who could shed light on enemy troop movements.

on a parallel track—experienced soldiers seldom move along unsecure trails—searching for a place to set up and monitor the path. Finding a suitable location, the rangers swung wide into the jungle to approach the trail from a different direction. They did this so as to leave no tracks close to the trail that might give away their location. The rangers set up their claymore mines near the trail and formed a small defensive circle 25 meters away.

The team had barely settled into place when 24 North Vietnamese regulars came along the trail. They wore khaki uniforms and carried AK-47 assault rifles and 107mm rockets. The presence of the rockets indicated they were preparing to assault a fixed American position. The nearby FSB Buttons seemed a likely target. Ranger Team 45 let them pass and then alerted headquarters.

A helicopter attack team hastened to the scene. For half an hour the choppers worked the area over. Tube artillery from the fire support base joined in. Just before dusk helicopters belonging to the aerial rocket artillery added their immense firepower. Later the rangers found 41 dead NVA soldiers in the target zone.

Since they hadn't been detected, the rangers continued to wait in ambush along the trail. Having completed part of their mission, they now wanted a prisoner so interrogation teams could learn details about the impending enemy attack. The five rangers stayed awake all night. At 2000 hours two NVA passed by, but again the rangers held their fire. Near dawn 10 more came along, their shadowy progress revealed by flares fired from the artillery base. Two hours later two soldiers passed carrying a litter, clearly the victim of the earlier ranger-directed bombardment. They were followed in another 35 minutes by 14 more NVA who also carried a litter with a wounded comrade. Within minutes two more came by. Sensing that the larger enemy forces had left the area, and since it was getting light, Sergeant Harvey decided to attack the next group passing through their kill zone. He requested helicopters to cover the team in the event he was wrong and a heavy contact occurred.

Minutes before 0700 hours the next morning, two more NVA approached the kill zone. As they entered, one of the rangers pressed the claymore's

detonator. Instead of the expected explosion the only result was a loud click as the detonator failed to make contact. The rangers froze, hoping the enemy would think the sound came from a large animal breaking a twig. One of the North Vietnamese soldiers peered carefully around, his AK-47 at the ready. He looked directly at one of the camouflaged rangers.

"He's seen me!" yelled the American.

Harvey immediately opened fire on full automatic with his M-16. The other rangers joined in while the claymore operator replaced the detonator and blew the mines.

The mines and rifle fire left one communist soldier dead on the trail. The other, wounded and bleeding badly, crawled off into the jungle. Two rangers pursued him while the rest of the team searched the dead soldier. The pursuit went slowly, visibility in the thick underbrush was less than five meters and they knew that somewhere out there was a wounded, dangerous enemy who could be lying in wait at any point. One of the rangers spotted a bush moving. He fired a snap burst and carefully approached. Nothing. The two hunters pulled back to join their comrades.

While the helicopters blasted the area where the wounded enemy soldier had disappeared, Ranger

PEASANT WEAPON: A Viet Cong guerrilla opens fire with an AK-47 near the ARVN ranger base at Trung Lap in 1971. Used by Communist insurgents worldwide, the easy-to-operate AK-47 has been dubbed "the peasant's weapon." With its 30-round banana clip it could be used like a sub-machine gun at close range and some US rangers favored captured versions to their own M-16 rifles.

Team 45 learned that an Air Cav reaction force was
coming to reinforce them. Waiting for their arrival
they heard sounds of men moving along the trail.
It was the point element of a larger enemy force.
From 40 meters away the rangers opened fire. To
disguise their small size the rangers blazed away
with all weapons. In particular, they hoped that the
sound of the M-14 rifle—a weapon, when used on full
automatic, that sounded much like an American
machine gun—would deceive the enemy into

The cowboys

CAPTURED:
Hands above his head, a Viet Cong suspect is ordered to the rear for interrogation after being routed from his hiding place by an ARVN ranger of the 21st Vietnamese Infantry Division. Once identified as a member of the Viet Cong, prisoners were offered a choice between imprisonment or undergoing a period of reindoctrination and training under the Chieu Hoi program. Those who chose the Chieu Hoi program were either resettled in safe villages or worked as Kit Carson scouts operating with US troops.

thinking they confronted a much bigger force. The enemy force deployed off the trail and returned fire. A heavy firefight erupted, exactly the kind of thing a small patrol wanted to avoid, but American reinforcements arrived to cover the team's retreat.

As the rangers and cavalrymen withdrew toward the clearing, one ranger and one trooper were hit. Carrying their wounded comrades, covered by a heavy helicopter bombardment, the Americans entered the clearing. Orders changed; instead of

pulling out they were to hold the clearing so more cavalry could come and join the battle. But, unable to close on the clearing because of the wall of fire the helicopters put down, the NVA broke contact. The rangers were extracted and a few minutes later reported to the intelligence officer at the fire support base.

During the debriefing certain aspects of the operation became clear. The mission showed the vulnerability of enemy forces to detection by ranger teams. No less than 55 NVA soldiers had passed within 20 meters of the concealed rangers and yet none had seen them. Excellent camouflage and noise discipline, the ability to remain completely silent in spite of extreme stress, prevented the premature disclosure of the ranger position. When they sprung their ambush, and the claymore misfired, the team had behaved with immense cool: first waiting to see if the enemy found them, then opening fire almost simultaneously when they realized their cover was blown.

Two small but important lessons came from the mission. In the future, claymore mines would be double primed to preclude misfires. Against a larger force the misfire could have been disastrous. Also, by reacting to an unexpected contact with high volumes of fire, the rangers bought valuable seconds while the enemy tried to figure out what they were up against. This gave time for reinforcements to arrive or for the rangers to break contact and escape.

Ranger Team 45's success involved both the battering of a hostile force and the detection of the enemy's plans. The next night a fully prepared FSB Buttons repulsed an NVA assault. The base credited the rangers for the timely alert. The report analyzing Ranger Team 45's ambush noted that the patrol behaved in the best ranger tradition. "The quality of young Skytroopers is clearly illustrated by this group of Rangers, averaging 20 years of age. They were confident of their abilities and aggressive in the application of their skills against the enemy."

Not all LRRP/ranger operations were nearly as successful as Ranger Team 45's mission. Many missions never found the enemy. Others collapsed in the face of skilled enemy reactions. In contrast to Ranger Team 45, poor planning coupled with inexperience placed a different ranger operation two months later in the A Shau Valley in extreme peril. It was to be a near disaster, a failure redeemed only by the surpassing bravery of some of the participants.

By then A Shau Valley had an evil reputation among American troops. From 1966, when the 1st Air Cavalry Division fought the first big battles between Americans and North Vietnamese regulars,

BACK TO SCHOOL:
Members of a Vietnamese ranger brigade board a helicopter to return to base for further assault training. Refresher courses could greatly enhance a unit's performance in the field.

The cowboys

CASUALTY OF WAR: His face contorted in pain, a Vietnamese ranger who lost his right hand in combat makes the long ride back to base for further medical treatment. The man, who proudly refused to lay on a stretcher, was one of thousands of Vietnamese rangers prepared to lay down their lives during the 21-year struggle to create a separate non-Communist state in South Vietnam.

until the war's end, the valley served as an important Communist stronghold. Frequently the Allies inflicted hard knocks on the enemy in the A Shau, but they always came back. On 24 January 1970, Ranger Team Polar Bear, Company L, 75th Rangers, went into the valley for another go.

Team Polar Bear consisted of a four-man and a five-man team. They ranged in age from 19 to 23 years. Some lacked the extensive combat experience that usually characterized ranger operations. With

hindsight, the complicated operational plan should have taken the men's inexperience into account.

The plan called for two helicopters to deliver the teams to an obscure hillside landing zone. Planners chose the LZ because helicopters could make a concealed approach up a valley followed by a sudden, hard right turn to the target. The officers directing the mission believed that the concealed approach would allow the rangers to surprise the enemy. Intelligence reports indicated that two elite North

Rotor effect —Tall swamp grass is momentarily flattened as US Army UH-1D helicopters drop down to discharge a ranger team. The tall grass made insertions and exfiltrations hazardous for both the rangers and the pilots.

Vietnamese sapper battalions occupied the area. The mission was to locate their base and capture prisoners. In order to sweep the most ground, the two teams would land at separate places and then move toward one another to link up. The least experienced team leader had the shortest distance to march to complete the linkup.

Whether entire armies or mere patrols are involved, maneuvering separate forces to join on the battlefield is hard to coordinate. In any event things went wrong from the beginning. The two helicopters lost sight of one another during the approach up the valley. The lead Huey had landed its team and lifted off before the second chopper arrived. With only seconds to go before he would set down, the pilot of the second Huey radioed for help, asking where he should land. No one could advise him so he set down in the general area where he thought the first team had landed.

The problem was that the "general area" became very large once the rangers actually touched down because, as the rangers jumped off the chopper's skids onto the ground, they found themselves swallowed up in a sea of six-foot-high elephant grass. Visibility was about as far as a man could reach. The second helicopter lifted off. Looking over the waves of elephant grass, the pilot spotted numerous trails crisscrossing the area. Along several of them came small groups of North Vietnamese soldiers.

He radioed his sighting to the ranger commander flying overhead in a command helicopter. The commander immediately realized his men were in trouble. His planned linkup was fouled by the fact that neither of the two teams knew where the other was located. It taxed their sense of direction merely to move about in blindingly tall elephant grass. And the NVA were on to them from the start.

The men on the ground immediately noticed movement. They saw the elephant grass bend and separate in an unnatural manner. Veteran French soldiers of an earlier war had learned to pause and listen when moving through elephant grass. The grass made a distinct crackle as it straightened upright after being bent back by the passage of humans. The inexperienced rangers didn't know this, so they wondered what caused the movement— the wind, animals, the other rangers, or the NVA.

Blundering along, one team came across signs of a recently placed minefield. This further slowed and distracted them. Meanwhile the other team stumbled onto a trail marked with footprints. While they were evaluating the significance of these marks, an eerie sound began that sent shivers down everyone's back. It was the sound of sticks clashing together and seemed to come from three different directions.

Suddenly a single shot broke the silence. Soon other single shots rang out as if in answer. Like the noise from the clashing sticks, the shots seemed to come from different directions and they seemed to move so as to surround the rangers. Both teams froze, uncertain what to do next. One ranger, looking across an overgrown garden plot, was certain he saw human movement. Watching intently he saw leaves rustle once and then again. He relaxed; it was the wind. Then the sticks started up again.

Another young ranger, on his first patrol, was shaking with fear. He gripped his rifle hard and prepared to fire at the sounds of movement that seemed to close in on him from all directions.

"Don't shoot," his sergeant hissed. "Look what you're aiming at." The ranger's weapon pointed directly at his own feet.

Overhead, the commander still tried to get the two

DIFFICULT TERRAIN: Men of C Company, 75th Rangers, work their way forward through elephant grass during an operation near Dalat in 1970. It was razor-sharp elephant grass, often taller than a man, that hampered Ranger Team Polar Bear as they tried to work their way to a landing zone as an NVA ambush team closed in.

teams to link up. He ordered the rangers to radio when they heard movement, figuring they were probably hearing one another. The commander tried to coordinate the movements and, failing that, tried to plot the teams' positions so he could direct them toward one another. It was impossible. The rangers couldn't tell who was making noise on the ground: the other team or the enemy. The only sure thing was that it wasn't Americans beating the sticks together.

The cowboys

HOMEMADE FRAG: A captured fragmentation grenade used by the Viet Cong as an antipersonnel weapon, discovered by ARVN rangers at Ly Van Manh. Made from a discarded tin can and filled with explosive and steel pellets, the grenade was lashed to a stick to make it easier to throw. The detonator trigger was wired down to prevent it from accidentally going off. For combat use, the wire was removed so that the lever would drop down on force of impact, plunging the detonator cap into the explosive.

Slowly the truth became apparent. The enemy was coordinating his movement with the noise from the sticks. It was primitive, yet in this environment it worked better than the rangers' radios. The telltale noise of the signal sticks indicated that the NVA had almost surrounded the two teams. But with visibility so restricted, they couldn't quite pinpoint the rangers' positions. The two team leaders made a decision, telling their men that regardless of what happened, "Don't fire 'cause they'll walk all over

The cowboys

BLINDFOLD:
An ARVN ranger holds a Viet Cong prisoner at gunpoint after he was discovered transmitting radio messages on ranger movements in the Trung Lap area. Situated in the heart of the Iron Triangle, the Communist stronghold close to the capital of Saigon, the ARVN ranger center at Trung Lap was a frequent target of enemy attacks.

us." The ranger commander realized the mission was hopelessly compromised. He turned his attention to getting his men out. Besides the terrain and the enemy, two things worked against him: Thick clouds were beginning to descend ominously and one of the two choppers had to leave its nearby orbit due to fuel shortage. Telling the rangers to forget about linking up, he ordered them to head for a clearing they had seen on the way in and prepare to be extracted. To cover them, the remaining helicopter swooped low in mock attack runs to keep the NVA occupied. It also dropped smoke grenades on the LZ, so the rangers could head in the right direction.

Getting out —Helicopter doorgunner's view of a ranger team with a Viet Cong prisoner, hands held high, rushing toward a helicopter for a quick departure after an operation in the Mekong Delta.

The rangers noticed that as the helicopter made its run, everything fell silent except for the roar of the chopper's engines. But once the helicopter completed its flyby, "the whole world started to move."

One of the experienced rangers thought the end was near. He'd seen much combat; the last few missions in particular had been full of enemy contacts. This time for sure, he thought, "we'd had it."

The two teams made it to within 35 and 100 meters, respectively, of the LZ. They couldn't get any closer because the elephant grass pulsed with enemy movement. One team leader made a crawling recon in the direction of some noise. He found crushed grass indicating the passage of considerable numbers of men. He knew it couldn't have been the other ranger team. Only then did he realize that the NVA were present in large numbers.

For three hours the members of Ranger Team Polar Bear remained surrounded and frozen in position. Cobra gunships arrived. Whispered radio directions from the ground managed to lead them against the enemy. The Cobras pelted the ground within 30 meters of the rangers. Only their fire kept the NVA at bay. Yet the stalemate couldn't last. The cloud cover cloaked the entire valley in a rapidly thickening fog. The ceiling was down to 200 feet. Time was on the side of the North Vietnamese.

The ranger commander made a decision. Since it was "starting to get dark, we had to get them out." He ordered Team Polar Bear to pop smoke grenades so he could pinpoint their positions. He knew the grenades would reveal them to friend and foe alike, but it had to be done. He requested helicopters for the extraction. Only one was available. Forced to

decide who might live and who might die, the commander made the tough decision which team to rescue. He chose the team trapped in a small gully, since the other rangers had the slight advantage of holding better ground.

The team leader learned that the rescue chopper was two minutes out. He told his men they would blast their way toward the landing zone using grenades. He led a grenade-hurling charge that reached the LZ. Amidst scattered enemy fire the

The cowboys

PADDY WAR: Small arms fire kicks up the water in a rice paddy as men of the 41st Vietnamese Ranger Battalion come under fire during operations in the Ca Mau Peninsula, Vietnam's southernmost point. An advance through an open rice paddy made an easy target for a Viet Cong sniper operating from the safety of a treeline. The ARVN rangers needed constant combat training by US advisors to improve their vigilance in the field.

Huey set down 50 meters away. They tried to scramble to the helicopter but the combination of thick, vine-covered underbrush, numerous small streams, and increasing hostile fire stopped them in their tracks, close to safety yet impossibly far away. They watched the empty helicopter lift off.

Rifle fire exploded from all around the clearing. Hard on its heels came the NVA assault. Only the Cobra's accurate fire kept the rangers from being immediately overrun. Waiting near the clearing

Safe marking —An ARVN ranger instructor shows how to place a marker to designate a landing zone. Standard procedure was to place a piece of light material in a hollowed-out area so that it could be seen from the air without being detected by the enemy on the ground.

they heard the splashing of many feet crossing a nearby stream. The North Vietnamese were closing in again. Braving intense ground fire, the helicopter pilot tried once more. He hovered just off the ground as the rangers pushed through the brush toward the craft.

The Huey made an unmistakable target. Numerous NVA soldiers blasted away at it. The rangers ignored the fire and tried to climb aboard. They had to jump to reach the helicopter's skids and then pull themselves up to climb aboard. Just as the first two balanced half in and half out, the helicopter shuddered from the impact of enemy fire. The violent motion pitched the rangers onto the ground. The intrepid pilot steadied the Huey, allowing the rangers to try again as friendly hands from the chopper reached out to assist them. A rocket-propelled grenade exploded nearby, wounding one of the rangers. With considerable effort he pulled himself aboard. The Huey lifted off. Half of Ranger Team Polar Bear were safe.

The enemy kept up the pressure against the five remaining rangers. They approached within 15 meters only to be beaten back by the Cobra gunships. It grew darker, making it increasingly difficult for the pilots to see the target. The Cobras' fire became wildly inaccurate. Emboldened, the NVA charged. In desperation, one of the rangers stood up amidst all the fire and held a strobe light so the pilot could clearly mark the ranger position. The Cobra immediately swooped low in a slow, accurate firing pass. The attackers went to the ground, foiled again.

In spite of the helicopter pilot's bravery and skill, the rangers felt it was only a matter of time before they were overrun. Soon the fog would eliminate any chance for extraction. They decided upon a last, desperate course of action. They would make a hell-for-leather charge through the underbrush to the landing zone. The M-79 grenadier led the way, firing blindly at any signs of movement.

Their surprise assault knocked the enemy off balance, miraculously permitting the rangers to reach the LZ. They lobbed white phosphorus grenades into the clearing to detonate any mines and to show their position to the fog-bound Huey circling somewhere overhead. The grenades did the job but they also clearly signposted the team's

EXTRACTION PROCEDURE: An ARVN ranger practices guiding a UH-1D helicopter into a landing zone after the pilot had located a ground marker (foreground left). The ability of helicopter pilots to land quickly in an LZ and extract troops under fire was often crucial to the success of ranger operations, as the men of Ranger Team Polar Bear discovered.

position to the North Vietnamese. Simultaneously the enemy infantry and the helicopter converged on the five rangers. Green tracer fire from AK-47s reached up into the swirling fog toward the rescue craft. Undaunted, the pilot steadily descended. Grenades and rifle fire exploded all around the rangers. While three men dashed through the fire toward the helicopter, the leader and assistant leader fought a two-man rearguard action.

The assistant team leader's grenade launcher jammed. Amidst wild NVA fire he calmly cleared his weapon and resumed firing. An enemy grenade toppled one of the three other rangers. His comrades helped him up and they boarded the Huey. The two remaining rangers backed toward the waiting chopper, methodically firing into the nearby treeline. They continued to shoot even as they climbed onto the skids and into the Huey. As the helicopter lifted off, numerous enemy soldiers emerged from the treeline. Standing in the flickering shadows caused by burning brush, firing from the hip, they stood in a circle surrounding the helicopter. Twenty-five meters away the Huey slowly rose into the now protective blanket of fog. It disappeared into the gloom. Ranger Team Polar Bear was safe.

Going home

10

An army in decline

BY 1970 the way the Allies fought the war had changed considerably. Everyone knew the Americans were going home. The burden of the fight would again be in the hands of the South Vietnamese.

An American advisor working with the 51st ARVN Ranger Battalion out along the Cambodian border recalls how the continuing US withdrawal seriously undermined his effectiveness. The South Vietnamese were less inclined than ever to listen to him. Furthermore, since the 51st participated in many forays over the border, and Americans were not permitted to accompany South Vietnamese troops on such missions, he became more of an observer than an advisor.

What he saw was an army in decline. The 51st never received a ranger-type mission. Instead South Vietnamese generals treated them like regular line units, using them to patrol just in front of the division during offensive sweeps and to plug gaps in the line during defensive operations. A South Vietnamese officer confirms the advisor's impression. He remembers that regardless of any specialized training, the rangers were used interchangeably with the Marine and airborne battalions.

Since the beginning the rangers had tended to be used this way. Yet by 1970 they still were more lightly equipped than regular infantry because their table of organization was based on the assumption that they would perform ranger-type operations. Thus they were outgunned when they encountered the North Vietnamese.

Even the quality of basic equipment remained uneven. In the 51st only the senior sergeants had combat boots; everyone else wore a kind of

Lone Ranger —Toting an M-79 grenade launcher and bearing a warning message, an ARVN ranger stalks a wounded VC in the jungle near the Cambodian border in November 1970. By this stage in the war the South Vietnamese rangers had begun to acquire considerable combat experience and the confidence that went with it.

high-topped sneaker. The quality of the personnel available to ranger units declined over time. Ranger recruiting stations set up in population centers and refugee camps tried hard to attract recruits by selling the elite image of the rangers.

But the word had spread about what being in the rangers really meant: 18 months out in the bush with only 15 days leave, a high risk of catching malaria, a likelihood of becoming involved in intense combat. So while many units maintained a cadre of very experienced sergeants and low-level officers, the bulk of the unit were just inexperienced draftees. The ranger battalions became ranger in name only.

Nonetheless, many South Vietnamese ranger battalions fought bravely. When North Vietnam launched its invasion of the South in 1972, ranger battalions were among the units thrown into the caldron of combat in a desperate struggle to stem the tide. It was no longer a guerrilla war. North Vietnamese tanks spearheaded massed infantry assaults supported by artillery.

The South Vietnamese had never before faced an armor assault. The same type of tank panic that afflicted the Allies in World War II when facing the Nazi blitzkrieg struck the ARVN defenders. Many soldiers threw down their weapons and ran in terror.

Into the breach went the 3d Ranger Group. Their advisor, Captain Harold Moffett, recalled the panic the tanks created. A few rangers tried to use their American-supplied light antitank weapons (LAW). When used at short range against the tank's vulnerable side and rear, the LAW could stop a tank. It required calm courage to let the tank draw near or even pass by before firing the LAW. Yet "word got around that a LAW would kill the tank. . . . Once the word spread it was just like wildfire. Everyone wanted to see how many tanks they could kill."

While many ran, many others didn't. In the 3d Ranger Group soldiers competed with one another to show who was the bravest, the most skillful, and who could destroy the most tanks. Remembering the spectacle of the rangers desperately battling to defend their country, the American advisor concluded that "they were gutsy little bastards."

Going home

ON THEIR OWN:
An ARVN ranger
captain issues
operational
orders and
briefs platoon
commanders
and Montagnard
guides on patrol
areas and
possible
ambush sites
before his men
embark on a
long-range
patrol into
enemy territory.
By the early
1970s ARVN
rangers like
these, who had
been used to
relying on US
advice and
firepower, had
to learn how to
fight on their
own.

AK-47	— Russian-designed Kalishnikov gas-operated 7.62mm automatic rifle with an effective range of 400m.
ARVN	— Army of South Vietnam.
B-52	— Eight-engine heavy bomber. The Boeing Stratofortress carried as many as 108 five-hundred-pound bombs per plane in support of the Marines at Khe Sanh.
CAR-15	— An early designation of the M-16 automatic rifle.
Claymore	— A command-detonated anti-personnel land mine that explodes in a 60-degree fan-shaped swath.
COSVN	— Central office for South Vietnam. Communist military and political headquarters for southern South Vietnam.
C-rations	— Standard-issue field rations.
E&E	— Escape and evasion.
FSB	— Fire support base.
Gun, 175mm	— Army weapon mounted on a tracked chassis and able to fire a 147-pound shell almost 33,000m max. Rate of fire is one round every two minutes.
Ho Chi Minh Trail	— The principal supply route from North to South Vietnam.
Huey	— Nickname for UH-1 series utility helicopter. Speedy and heavily armed, it was used to support larger, more vulnerable helicopters.
KIA	— Killed in action.
Kit Carson scouts	— Viet Cong defectors, recruited by marines to serve as scouts, interpreters, and intelligence agents.
L-19	— Military version of the Cessna C-37, otherwise known as the 0-1 Birddog.
LRP	— Long-range patrol.
LRRP	— Long range reconnaissance patrol —interchangeable with LRP.
LZ	— Landing zone: usually a small

clearing secured temporarily for the landing of resupply helicopters. Some became more permanent and eventually became base camps.

MACV — Military Assistance Command, Vietnam. US command for all US military activities in Vietnam.

Mortar, 4.2-inch — A large mortar with a rifled bore and a range of 4,000m. The shell has in its base a soft metal that expands into the rifling when the propellant explodes.

Mortar, 60mm — Smooth-bore, muzzle-loaded weapon used by both the Americans and North Vietnamese. It has an effective range of about 2,000m.

Mortar, 81mm — Marine weapon resembling the 60mm type. It propels a larger shell for an effective range up to 3,650m.

MP — Military police(men).

NVA — North Vietnamese Army. Often used colloquially to refer to North Vietnamese soldier in the same way as "ARVN" was used to designate a South Vietnamese soldier.

Rifle, M-16 — US infantry weapon. It weighs only 7.6 pounds, uses a 5.62mm cartridge, and is capable of semi-automatic or fully automatic operation.

Sapper — VC commando, usually armed with explosives.

Tet — The lunar New Year.

Tet Offensive — The surprise attack by the North Vietnamese in May 1968.

VC — Viet Cong.

War Zone C — Military designation of the area between Saigon and the Cambodian border that was heavily infiltrated by the Viet Cong.

WIA — Wounded in action.

About the author

James R. Arnold

James R. Arnold is a freelance writer who has contributed to numerous military journals and is the author of a history of the US Army Corps of Engineers' role in the Lincoln Memorial. He wrote *Armor* and *Artillery* for the *Illustrated History of the Vietnam War* series.

A specialist on the Napoleonic campaigns, he has written on Napoleon's marshals and is writing a study of Napoleon's 1809 campaign. He is also writing a historical novel about the Civil War, centered on the Blue Ridge Mountains near Berryville, Virginia, where he lives.

Born in 1952 in Harvey, Illinois, James R. Arnold spent his formative years overseas and used the opportunity to study the sites of famous battles. Tours of Normandy and the Ardennes, coupled with a visit to Paris for Napoleon's bicentennial, prompted him to pursue historical study. Encouraged by scholars at the UK's Sandhurst Military Academy, he had his first work published in the British Journal of the Society for Army Historical Research.

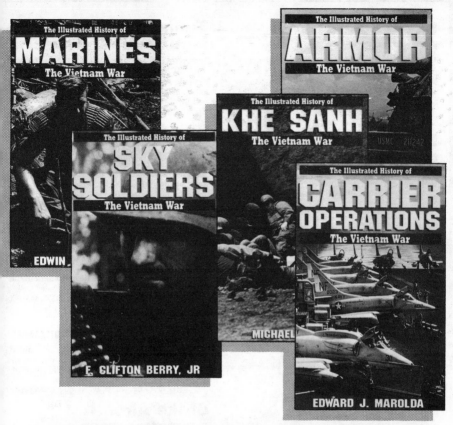

The Illustrated History of
MARINES
The Vietnam War
EDWIN

The Illustrated History of
ARMOR
The Vietnam War
USMC 21242

The Illustrated History of
KHE SANH
The Vietnam War

The Illustrated History of
SKY SOLDIERS
The Vietnam War
F. CLIFTON BERRY, JR

The Illustrated History of
CARRIER OPERATIONS
The Vietnam War
EDWARD J. MAROLDA

MICHAEL

THE ILLUSTRATED HISTORY OF THE VIETNAM WAR

Bantam's Illustrated History of the Vietnam War is a unique and new series of books exploring in depth the war that seared America to the core: A war that cost 58,022 American lives, that saw great heroism and resourcefulness mixed with terrible destruction and tragedy.

The Illustrated History of the Vietnam War examines exactly what happened: every significant aspect—the physical details, the operations and the strategies behind them—is analyzed in short, crisply written original books by established historians and journalists.

Some books are devoted to key battles and campaigns, others unfold the stories of elite groups and fighting units, while others focus on the role of specific weapons and tactics.

Each volume is totally original and is richly illustrated with photographs, line drawings, and maps.